101 Ways

To Get Your Progressive Issues On

TALK
RADIO

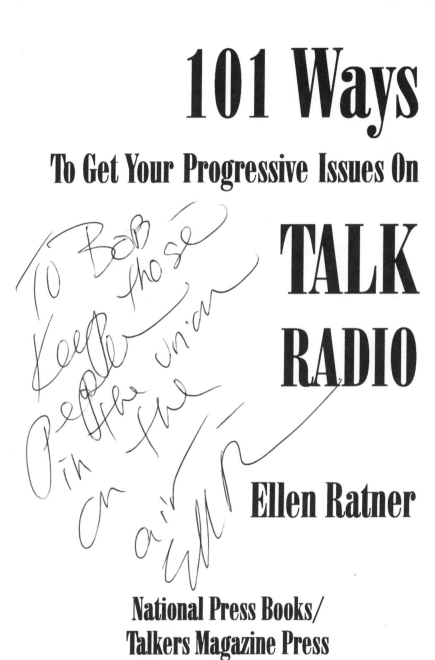

To Bob
keep those
people in the union
on the
air
Ellen

Ellen Ratner

National Press Books/
Talkers Magazine Press

Library of Congress Cataloging in Publication Data

Ratner, Ellen, 1951—
101 ways to get your progressive issues on talk radio
Ellen Ratner.
192 pp. 15 cm x 23 cm
Includes bibliographical references and index.
ISBN 1-882605-31-4 (hardcover)
ISBN 1-882605-32-2
1. Radio in politics--United States.
2. Talk shows--United States.
3. Advertising, Political--United States.
I. Title.
HE8689.7 P6R38   1997
324.7'3'0973--dc21   96-51804
CIP

PRINTED IN THE UNITED STATES OF AMERICA

To my brothers, Michael and Bruce, who have spent the last 45 years educating me in the progressive tradition and to the memory of WGY's Paul Cassidy (Eric Schwartz), a great broadcaster and a good friend.

"For all of their shortcomings, the popularity of Limbaugh and the other talk radio jockeys transcends the matter of ideology. Their success reflects a public thirst for debate and argument that goes beyond the confines usually imposed by conventional definitions of news. The lesson that Limbaugh offers—both to his critics and to the conventional media—is not that all should copy his style of argument, but that argument itself is much in demand."

—E.J. Dionne, Jr.,

They Only Look Dead: Why Progressives Will Dominate the Next Political Era

Acknowledgments

This book began after many long conversations with Doug Stephan, host of *Good Day U.S.A* and co-host of the *Good Day U.S.A.'s* "Washington Reality Check." After many terrible progressive guests, we began talking about what could be done to improve the quality of progressive arguments. Several people spent time looking over the manuscript: Aric Caplan, Kathie Scarrah, Bob Newman, and Celia Rocks. They gave me their time and many valuable suggestions. Throughout the last few years, while they were at the Democratic National Committee, Lesley Gold and Noah Shachtman helped me develop many of the ideas contained in this book.

I had wonderful and extremely helpful discussions with Rick Mangus, Janet Parshall, Joe Madison, Jim Bohannon, Barry Lynn, Allida Black, E.J. Dionne Jr., Howard Kurtz, Richard Miller, Paul Rodriquez, Mary Beal, Michael Reagan, Frankie Boyer, Stella Harrison and Darla Shine.

Civil servants sometimes do not get the credit they deserve, but several govenment employees have gone above and beyond the call of duty when it comes to radio. First and foremost, Rica Rodman at the White House knows the ins and outs of radio and is the best example of someone who works hard as an advocate the talk medium. In addition, Leah Levin, Dan Israel and Jay Byrne were extremely helpful. Richard Strauss, now working in the private sector, worked hard to bring talk radio to the White House.

Denni Robi helped organize and edit the first draft and provided expertise about the use of actualities.

Susan Messina edited the final manuscript. Her suggestions were particularly insightful. Charlotte Haynes also helped in proofing the manuscript.

My radio partners Kandy Stroud and Mike Sponder continue to be helpful. Carla Darby helped when we were on deadline.

Andrew Barlow, Marc Wittlif, and Mike Johnson have all given valuable input.

I would also like to thank Sam Miller, Maria Miller, Theone Mark, Laurie Weiner, Anna Donovan, Brook Stroud, Allison Miller, Victor Kovner, Sarah Kovner and Paula Krulak.

It really does takes a village to write a book . . . Mario Brossard of *The Washington Post* ran additional data on his research, the folks at Edison Research worked to get us their 1996 data, Mollyann Brodie at the Kaiser Family Foundation was patient with our requests. The Pew Research Center staff is the was fast and efficent each time I made a request. I want to also thank Paragon Research as well as the Radio Advertising Bureau for sharing the Simmons Research material. Yanlovich let us use the *Time-CNN* data, and Lee C. Shapiro of Voter's News Service was quick and helpful with their data. Thank's also to The November group for helping us out and the Annenberg School at the University of Pennsylvania for providing essential data.

Four people from the Republican side of life have been great: Jeff Dickerson, Scott Hoganson, Lauren Maddox, and Leigh LaMora.

Thanks also to Laurie McHugh, Barry Toiv, Mary Ellen Glynn, Fred Clark, Maryanne Krayer, Mel Pohl, Wayne Knoll, Frank Stroud, Vicki Daley, Barbara Shaver, Patricia Stranahan, Alice Fontanez, Armand Barbaria, Bunny Starr, Edith and Henry Everett, April Mellody, Kathy McKiernnen, David Paulsen, Connie Lawn, Trude Feldman, Mary Krayer, Donna Singleton, Sherri Marton, Helen Soski, Mark Bosswick, Ann Jones, Carl Abrams, Randall Hodson, Conchita Balinong, Bud Aiello, Michelle Mederios, Robert Vanasse, Marilyn Yarus, Joan Biando, Jill Notini, Jason Notini, Brenda Notini, Ellen Donnelly, Matt Flox, Dan Shapiro, Neel Lattimore, Nancy Robinson, Christine Krithades, Caitlin Ryan, Dr. Michael Hamilton and the folks at the Duke Diet and Fitness Center, Carol Nashe at NARTSH, Jerry Mazzuchi of Legi-Slate, John Garrison, who kept me walking, Dr. Gerald Pitman, who made me look and feel younger, and Michael Gotwald and Michael Finch for their great decor.

Scout of Basile-Ryan made the statistics look great, Christian Capobianco helped me with important interviews, Eric Berman, for his research and Jared McGarrity, Debra Murry, Terry Ciulla, and Jeanne

Oates Angulo. Anne Gehman got me started and Jeff Clothy provided insight for talk radio audiences.

The following radio hosts helped me with information and comments, including Armstrong Williams, Blanquita Cullum, Mark Johnson, Jeff Brucculeri, Steve Bowers, Jon Anderson, Scott Henning, Rick Minyard, Howard Monroe, Steve Chaconas, Les Kinsolving, Dave Anthony, Tom Rheinstein, Joe Clark, Joe Scialfa, Tom Parker, David Lile, Jim Marshall, Paul Begosian, Curt Hahn, David Payne, Connie Lawn, Sarah McClendon, Danny Jones, Pat Desmaris, Bruce Gordon, Howard Miller, Andy Wolfe, Wayne Cannon, David Payne, Simon Rose, Dan Corkery, Wyatt Cox, Roger Fredenberg and Dom Giordano.

My family, Michael and Bruce, Julie, Karen, Rebbie, Lizzie, Hugo and Charlotte have always been a support to me in my radio and writing career. Thanks also to Jake, Ana, Leora, Eli, Caroline and Pesha, for making me smile.

Susan Haynes made sure I was well-taken care of during the Blizzard of '96, when the bulk of this book was written.

Michael Harrison supported this project from the get-go and fortunately put his fine editorial hand on this book. Sharon and Matthew Harrison lent a helping hand as well.

Table of Contents

Foreword

Michael Harrison

As editor and publisher of *Talkers Magazine,* the trade publication in the talk radio business, I have spent a lot of time during the past seven years trying to convince the outside world that there's a lot more to talk radio than partisan Republican conservative politics. This exaggerated perception exists because of the shadow cast across the mainstream media canvas by several of talk radio's highest-profile practitioners namely, Rush Limbaugh, but in fact, the medium is far more diverse than that. So much so that we at *Talkers Magazine* have had to be especially careful to take as politically neutral a position as possible in order to remain a credible vehicle for the entire industry an industry popularized by some of the most opinionated, self-assured and uncompromising forces in American mass media. In other words, they jump all over us when we start showing sides.

So we stick to our main job of being proponents of the free marketplace of ideas and the First Amendment, celebrating all the voices that are heard and have yet to be heard in this exciting form of communication.

In this regard, I guess my work has turned me into somewhat of a radical moderate.

Be that as it may, in spite of my protestations to the contrary and clearly the mixed results of the latest elections, the perception still exists that conservatives own talk radio and that the liberals are the outsiders being denied the power of one of the great persuasive forces in the propaganda universe.

Thus, when my left-leaning colleague, Ellen Ratner, came to me with the idea of publishing a book focusing on the essence of her vast knowledge of how this media works toward detailing what a liberal publicist, political candidate, organization or operative can do to make its vast resources work for them, I welcomed it as a much needed tool for balancing the playing field.

Although there has been an expansion of the political parameters in talk radio over the past couple of years (especially 1996), many left-of-centers still believe that they have a long way to go before they can fully tap the benefits of this free pipeline into the minds of broadcasting's most politically-active audience.

With that in mind, I didn't put up (much of) an argument against using the word "progressive" (an apologetic euphemism for 'liberal') in the title of this book, although I personally believe that its message will be of equal value to conservatives. It might even be of service to radical moderates like me who have the courage to face the charge of being wishy-washy in an artificially polarized environment instigated by the sound-bite crazy mainstream media.

Not to mention the more players the merrier, a goal that can only add to the validity of our assessment that, when taken as a whole, talk radio is the most accurate bellwether of American public opinion in the mass media today.

1

Introduction

At the Talk Radio New Service, we've become convinced that talk radio functions as America's front porch and backyard— and that progressives must learn to effectively use the power of talk radio shows.

People use talk radio to discuss issues that are vital to them, to their families and to their communities, just like Americans once sat around on porches or hung over back fences to gossip, discuss, disagree and laugh. Talk radio is where many Americans go to chew over anxieties, concerns and even outrages with like-minded individuals—as well with people who disagree with them.

In today's fragmented society, where people often live in anonymous communities, far from their families, talk radio has become an important way for people to connect to others. People are searching for answers to their pain, uncertainty and frustration and they turn to talk radio to address those issues. A talk host's job is to address those issues by asking guests the very questions that are in the audience's mind. The host functions essentially as the moderator of a town meeting.

Janet Parshall, a conservative radio talk show host, points out that talk radio is a profoundly intimate medium because talk show hosts choose topics and guests that mirror the day-to-day concerns of their listeners. Talk radio's intimacy stems from the fact that it attempts to meet people's needs for information and solace in a complex and often scary world. Talk show host Joe Madison notes that radio is a particularly intimate medium because hosts and guests are in listeners' homes and the front seat of their cars.

We also agree with Parshall's assertion that radio's interactive component makes it a powerful medium. People argue with their radios, talk back, gesticulate with their hands. Radio hosts are familiar with callers who say, "I had to phone in because I've just been screaming in my car at what that last person just said." Listeners to radio programs are actively engaged in responding to the material being presented. Talk host Madison states that effective radio guests, particularly if they are politicians, must engage with their audience and with the host. He cites President Clinton as a politician who is good on the radio because of his ability to banter with the host. "Listening to Clinton and [Don] Imus together is fun; it's like they grew up together," he notes.

The entire talk radio business is a stimulus-response enterprise. A stimulus, in the form of hot news, a provocative guest or an important ongoing debate, is presented to the listeners and then the response begins. Sometimes the response is a call to the show, or a discussion later with a friend: "Hey, I heard something on the radio today that I couldn't believe. . ." Other times, listeners' responses are more wide-reaching and move into the realm of social and political action:

- Writing checks to charities or political action committees;
- Contacting federal and state representatives;
- Boycotting products;
- Attending town meetings
- Organizing advocacy campaigns;
- Participating in rallies or protests; and
- Voting.

Clearly, the results of the 1994 elections showed us all the power of conservative talk show hosts and programs. Industry insiders and political operators are convinced that talk radio played just as big a role—if not bigger—in the 1996 elections, not so much with the national elections, but definitely with the local elections where many debates were held on local talk radio stations. As political consultant Bob Shrum says: "A political rally in California is two people sitting in front of their TV sets." The same goes for radio. It's imperative that progressives harness the power of talk radio and stop allowing the right wing to control effective use of this powerful medium.

Why have progressives lost the airwaves war? There are two categories of reasons. The first is the progressives' fault. By and large progressives gave up the fight and ceded victory to the conservatives who are masters at using radio to their advantage. Many liberal organizations and spokespeople dismiss radio audiences as too conservative to bother with, setting up a situation in which only conservative voices get regular airplay.

Most progressives are too earnest to be entertaining. Face it: progressives are bolstered by the utter conviction that they are morally right about social and economic issues. It's not that progressives don't have the moral high ground—we believe they do— but, as Howard Kurtz, media critic for the *Washington Post* says, most progressives lack a sense of humor and so can appear self-righteous and boring. Radio is, after all, a for-profit, entertainment industry. That which is lively, entertaining and enjoyable sells advertising time and turns a profit. As football player John Riggins said to Justice Sandra Day O'Connor, "Loosen up, baby, you're too tight."

Although the television news folks try to downplay the value of talk radio, the television evening news is also moved by ratings. That is the reason that the 11 p.m. news often begins with a teaser about the latest murder—it sells.

Progressives are worried about offending others. Talk host Mark Weaver says, "Due to liberals' nature, they're too kind and worried about saying something that someone would take offense at." He adds, "Don't be afraid to be irreverent . . . a liberal could be just as successful as Rush Limbaugh, you just need to be a good performer."

Boring doesn't sell. Policy wonks droning on about details of complex programs don't sell. Progressives live in a marshmallow swamp. "They have trouble posing issues as succinctly as possible, often because they see both sides of an issue" notes Barry Lynn, a radio host who is also the Executive Director of Americans for the Separation of Church and State. Radio host Jim Bohannon observes," Liberals need to have a little more of a chip on their left shoulder."

Progressives have had a tough time coming up with a clear economic agenda to impart. Americans care deeply about their own economic security and future. Progressives must make policy issues relevant to Mr. or Ms. Smiths' wallets in real and concrete ways.

The second set of reasons that conservatives dominate radio is linked to the fundamentally conservative nature of radio and the businesses that buy advertising time. An all-liberal talk show is unlikely to work. Why? Howard Kurtz explains that stations in small to medium-sized markets would have a very hard time selling advertisers on the idea. Small business advertising revenue provides the backbone of much of America's radio stations. Small businesses are generally unwilling to advertise their product or service on a show that they perceive as too far out of the mainstream.

For the same reason, most stations won't air shows featuring hosts with really left opinions. Too risky. Thus, it is up to guests—informed, articulate, progressive guests—to balance the conservative leaning of most hosts.

This book is designed to help you get your progressive issues, campaigns, and spokespeople on the air. The following pages include 101 tried and true tips, gleaned from the best minds in talk radio, to help you take a seat right on America's front porch and backyard through radio. You'll find strategies for:

- Preparing your message and campaign;
- Marketing the campaign, the issue or your spokesperson;
- Booking your spokesperson;
- Cultivating relationships with producers and hosts
- Being an effective on-air spokesperson;
- Proper after-show follow-up; and
- Using the Internet to get your message out.

You'll also find important statistics about talk radio listeners, a simple check off form to keep your campaign on track and a resource list for further assistance.

The bottom line is this: as progressives, we care about truth, justice and making the world a healthier, more fair and compassionate place. We have to take progressive messages to the air in a way that people will understand and respond to. We won't change the hearts and minds of the most right wing conservatives, but there is a huge middle segment on almost every social and economic issue that can be swayed by correct information, gripping stories and articulate, charismatic spokespeople. Cal Thomas says, "The mushy middle's big decision is what video to rent on Friday night. They don't engage issues—so sounding good and [touching] feelings are important." The intimate medium of talk radio is ideal for touching middle America while waking up, driving to or from work or just before retiring for the evening. Talk radio has become America's companion, a friendly voice that can be used to introduce progressive ideas to a receptive and captive audience.

2

Pre-Test

Answer each question TRUE or FALSE?:

1. In-studio interviews work as well as telephone interviews. TRUE or FALSE?

2. It is more important to get your issue across than it is to be likable. TRUE or FALSE?

3. You will be able to tell immediately if a radio campaign is effective. TRUE or FALSE?

4. It's okay for a call-in listener to lie to get past a screener. TRUE or FALSE?

5. If you are on the morally correct side of an issue, your message is bound to be convincing. TRUE or FALSE?

6. It's a mistake to tie your issue to current events because it makes your issue appear trendy and not substantial. TRUE or FALSE?

7. Doing weekend radio programs is a waste of time. TRUE or FALSE?

8. Talk radio audiences are predominantly conservative. TRUE or FALSE?

9. A good way to establish rapport with a talk show host is to ask about the host's personal political beliefs. TRUE or FALSE?

10. Making jokes during a show is a bad idea because it demonstrates that you're not serious. TRUE or FALSE?

ANSWERS

1. False. See # 90, page 119.

2. False. See # 20, page 48.

3. False. See # 11, page 39.

4. False. See # 36, page 67.

5. False. See # 12, page 40.

6. False. See # 10, page 38.

7. False. See # 41, page 73.

8. False. See statistics section, page 153-182.

9. False. See # 57, page 89.

10. False. See # 84, page 113.

3

Preparing the Message and the Campaign

There is a reason that conservatives are winning the radio war: They are always willing to get on the air.

One conservative activist said, "If a station is five watts, I'm there" while a spokesperson on the left said, "I won't do single station shows, I only get on syndicated shows." That sums up the difference. Small stations add up and create a critical mass. Their listeners tend to be very loyal. They are impressed if a bigwig is willing to do an interview on their little station. Be willing to go the extra mile and get on the air. If enough folks with a progressive viewpoint were on the air then radio would not be dominated by the conservative viewpoint. One host inquired about having a well known president of an airline on. The host was told that the president's schedule was booked one year in advance. No one is that busy, not even the President of the United States.

One government official said, "We only do shows heard inside the beltway (the perimeter road around Washington, D.C.). We like to hear our work."

A radio interview can take as little as five minutes.

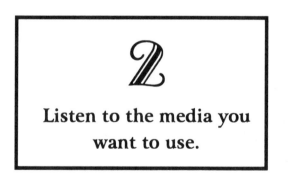

2

Listen to the media you want to use.

If your goal is to get on talk radio, listen to the shows that are broadcast in your area as well as those that are nationally syndicated. Many syndicated shows are now available via satellite and many home dishes can access them. If radio news is your goal, listen to the hourly news on the stations in your area as well as the "all-news" networks. Morning drive is an important time for radio so listening to the "morning zoo" formats is beneficial. Don't forget about weekend specialty shows. Listen to the guests on these shows and note what makes you listen. There is a radio test, "the drive test," that asks: "Can a topic capture your attention while you are driving to and from work with other things on your mind?"

If you are listening to the host's show that you are going to be on, be sure to listen to the style, voice and cadence of the host. Revise the style of the spokesperson accordingly. Be sure that the spokesperson is listening to the station as they are getting dressed, getting ready to leave for the station, in the car etc. Most hotels have radios and many stations are live on the Internet so it is possible to hear a show even if it is located in a different city.

While listening, have your spokesperson listen to the guest and practice his or her responses , pretending that he or she is the guest.

If you are planning an immediate on-air campaign, listen to the issues of the week. We live in a culture that responds to trends and we tend to have a pack mentality. You want to make sure that your literature and your spokesperson are aware of the mood and theme of the country as well as the demographics and lifestyle of the people you are trying to reach. The goal is to dovetail your issues to current trends so that they sound timely.

Define your issue. Create your message.

Make a list of the toughest questions you can think of pertaining to your issue, especially the ones you don't want to answer. This is the best way to begin your campaign because these are the questions that will likely be asked on the air. If you can answer the toughest questions, you are prepared to debate your issues with conservative friends. (If you don't have any conservative friends, get some; they don't have horns.) This will help you to develop both your printed material and your on air campaign.

Make sure you answer two important questions: "How does this affect Joe and Sally's pocketbook?" and "Does this issue fit into Joe and Sally's value system?" For example, on the issues of AIDS and homosexuality, the Far Right sees homosexuality as a moral issue and nothing is going to change that. However, when the cost of condoms and sex education is compared to the costs of treating the AIDS epidemic, many Americans see the logic provided you are careful to acknowledge their values.

In defining your message make sure that you are not using the negative phrases that your host or opposition uses when he or she speaks to you. It will reinforce listener stereotypes. The National Education Association doesn't let their opposition pigeon hole it with words such as "school violence." They prefer to use the words "safe schools." Change the language, change the perception.

4

Use popular expressions and images.

Senator Jesse Helms, in his quest to remake the State Department, released daily faxes borrowing on Rush Limbaugh's "America Held Hostage." Several recent media campaigns have been based on David Letterman's Top Ten lists. Takeoffs of Christmas carols were read on the air during the government shutdown. PETA (People for the Ethical Treatment of Animals) posted signs reading: "Thanksgiving is Murder on Turkeys."

And let's not forget Senator Al D'Amato singing a Whitewater song to the tune of Old MacDonald in the Senate chambers, complete with a large poster of a pink pig. Everyone thought D'Amato was a buffoon, but EVERY network carried it.

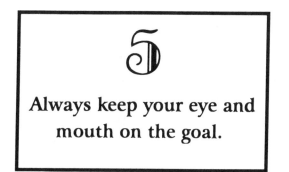

5

Always keep your eye and mouth on the goal.

Design a goal that is measurable and obtainable. Consider carefully exactly what you want to accomplish with this campaign. Have a 24-hour plan of action as to what will be accomplished in any one "news day." P.R. executive Bob Newman organized a campaign to help keep Social Security intact. He set a goal with his client to turn around certain states, blanketing them with television and radio. The goal of his campaign was to saturate certain state's delegations. Everything the spokesperson said, every media appearance was designed to keep pressure on certain congressional districts. It worked. One of the main reasons that President Bill Clinton has resonated with the electorate is because he is like a radio program director looking for audience issues and demographics, he wants to find out what works. You should be doing the same BEFORE you get your issue on the radio.

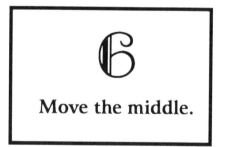

Move the middle.

A certain number of listeners will vote/buy and espouse the conservative agenda. A smaller number will vote/buy and espouse the liberal agenda. Your aim is to move the middle and so your entire presentation should be geared to these people. Playing to anyone else is just dead air and a waste of time. It is important, however, when playing the middle that you do not turn your back on your core constituency. Be careful, because if you alienate this group they will not vote with your issue in mind and not support your cause financially.

There is a reason that the newspaper *USA Today* sells so well. It is designed to speak to the common denominators of American Life. If you want to know what folks are talking about , do some street research in the pool halls, bowling alleys and beauty shops. Things that interest you may not interest the average Sam or Sally and may not speak to where they live.

During the 1996 Presidential Debates, President Clinton did well because he knew who he was speaking to. In the town hall format, the questions of the audience did not focus on any of the controversy surrounding the President. The questions focused on pocketbook issues. Issues that concerned paying the bills and personal safety and security. You will need to adapt your angle and message to your audience. Translated that means know your audience.

Mike Sponder, who often beats the pundits with his predictions, had an interesting analysis of the middle voter. Basically, Bob Dole received 41% of the popular vote. Most of Dole's vote, probably 35% of the electorate, are straight-line Republicans, so at most six percent of the Republicans split their ticket when voting for Congress. Of the Clinton voters, if each of those who voted for Clinton cast their votes for Congressional Democrats, it would account for the entire Democratic vote. Of course there were the Perot voters, but the election polls support Sponder's theory.

The Pew Research poll shows that only eight percent of the voters split their tickets. The Voters News Service data concurs. Why then is the middle so important? One grocery store that dominates the

Washington, D.C. market, started in the 1930s as a family operation. As it grew family members began to fight. It was decided to give each faction 49% of the voting stock and a trusted family friend was given two percent. Sixty years later which ever family group gets the two percent owner on their side controls the company. The middle may not be great in numbers, but it can control the direction of the country.

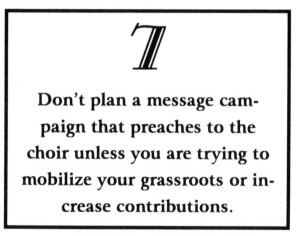

7

Don't plan a message campaign that preaches to the choir unless you are trying to mobilize your grassroots or increase contributions.

With issues such as abortion, where there is very little that will change opinions, your media campaign might be for the sole purpose of keeping the issue alive in the hearts, minds and pocketbooks of your supporters. If you are using your media campaign to mobilize your supporters, be sure that your message is finely honed to get your desired results.

Answer the questions:

- Do you want contributions?
- Do you need volunteers?

• Are you interested in letting your core supporters know what you are doing?

Unless you have a clear goal in addressing your supporters, don't spend useful time preaching to the choir. Instead, spend it talking to your non-supporters. Bob Dole's daughter admitted on the air that she is pro-choice. The effect of her admission was to soften Dole's hard line anti-abortion image and make him more appealing to middle-of-the-road voters. Ultimately, it didn't turn around his presidential campaign, but it helped keep some women voters on the Republican ship.

Sometimes preaching to the choir may mean moving them to the middle. During the 1996 elections, Congressman Barney Frank encouraged the gay community to vote for Clinton. "Voting is not dating" he said, meaning that you can not find perfection by voting.

Make your issue personal.

Can people identify with your issue or your spokesperson? Paint a picture with words and make sure there is something in it that people can identify with. Randy Weaver, the white separatist, garnered public sympathy because people could identify with his fear of being the "little guy" overwhelmed by the federal bureaucracy and federal gun power. During one of the 1995 federal government shutdowns, a radio station had several"non-essential" workers on the air to tell why their jobs were, in fact, essential.

Ask yourself, can people identify your issue with its impact on women, children and families? Whenever possible, put their faces on every topic, from the Oklahoma City bombing to the UNABOMBER to Nicole Brown Simpson.

It is important when making your issue personal, however, that it just doesn't focus on "I." Make it clear that there is a "we." Say things like "our members tell us."

9

Make complex situations understandable.

The conflicts in Bosnia and Rwanda are examples of stories that were glossed over in the news but could have gotten more play on talk shows if the issues were presented differently. Americans, overwhelmed with their own lives, couldn't deal with the sheer volume of the genocide in Rwanda and Bosnia. To make the Bosnian connection more real, American rescue workers could have told their story and explained what moved them to spend time in the war zone. In the early days of the Bosnian conflict, it was just too complex until there was a threat of American troops and American dollars. The story could have been made more understandable by using American terms and metaphors that are closer to home, such as the relationship of Quebec to Canada. Whenever possible, talk about a population or land area in terms that Americans can visualize. In this example you could say "A country as small as New Jersey." Also, use a situation at home that compares similar conflicts like that between Koreans and African-Americans. Use something that makes the situation identifiable.

10

Piggyback your issue on hot news and current events.

Do the homework to find books about to be published, movies that are about to be released, and recent magazine and newspaper features relevant to your campaign/issue. Your issue will have more clout and relevance if it's tied to some hot news. If you are planning a local campaign, identify something on a national level can be tied to the local situation and an event.

If a relevant and hot story breaks, clear your spokesperson's schedule so that he or she can be available to respond. Kathie Scarrah, a media expert from Senator Lieberman's office suggests, "Don't be a media pig, but be willing to really work with the media."

Consider these examples of an issue tagging along with news or a TV show.

- The revelation of Nicole Simpson's abuse by O.J. Simpson brought the issue of domestic violence into the spotlight.

- Candace Gingrich's revelation that she is a lesbian has been very useful to Gay and Lesbian civil right's groups. No stranger to good public relations campaigns, they have used this revelation by Newt Gingrich's sister to further their campaign.

- Lucille Ball starred in a made-for-television movie on homelessness. During the commercial breaks, local shelters and homeless groups were able to give information about their programs.

11

Give time to make something work.

Talk radio doesn't work on a 24-hour news cycle. It works on repetition and continuous plugging. While an occasional issue (such as Zoe Baird and Nannygate or the House Bank checking account overdraft scandal) will produce an immediate reaction, most campaigns take real saturation and blanketing of the markets. One member of Congress who put a new weekly feature on radio wanted to know why he hadn't received much reaction after just a month. Radio involves continuous input if you want long-lasting results.

The flip side of this is that talk radio can keep an issue alive long after other media have dropped it. For example, Senator Lieberman launched a campaign called "Cleaning Up Trash TV" that talk radio picked up and used for several weeks. Because there was so much radio-generated response to this issue, Geraldo voluntarily issued the "Ten Commandments on How to Treat Guests."

It's important, however, to keep reinventing your message with new angles. You can't just keep recycling the same old stuff and expect to see results. As media consultant Aric Caplan points out, "TV is limited by the size of the screen. Magazines and newspapers have detail and graphics but lack timeliness. Talk radio is limited only by a listener's interest in a topic." Keep that interest alive with fresh information.

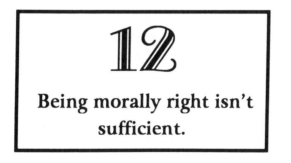

12

Being morally right isn't sufficient.

Be able to offer alternates that reduce people's fears and don't intrude on people's lives. The Clinton health care plan went down simply because it scared people and the Republicans were able to exploit that. They were able to prey on the fear of too much government control in the lives of ordinary people and to make hay out of too many closed doors. The Clinton heath care plan seemed beyond the reach and understanding of most average Americans and the debate never focused on the simple, pocketbook issues for individuals and for the nation. Furthermore, a major controversy on talk radio has been the FDA's position on the efficacy of vitamins, supplements, and alternative therapies. While there may be reasonable scientific questions about the value of these alternatives, listeners perceived the issue as another example of government influence on choice and freedom. One of the operative concepts is control. Do the listeners perceive that they will be more in control of their lives with your plan or issue or less? Will someone else have the control or will they have the control?

Another effective strategy is to agree with callers. If the caller doesn't like foreign aid, you can begin the first question by agreeing with the caller. "I think there is a lot of evidence to support your views, but let me give you some other facts." This takes you off the moral stance and allows the other person to be right, but keeps you in control of the interview.

13

Timing is crucial.

Many a great air campaign has been ruined due to timing. There are obvious dead times such as the week of the Fourth of July, Christmas, Labor Day and so on (unless your issue fits into such themes). But you should also pay attention to what else is going on. If your issue is political, it is easier to get attention when Congress is in session. On the other hand, there are times when it is worth pulling a campaign to wait out a dominating issue such as the opening and verdict of the O.J. Simpson trial, the Oklahoma City bombing and so on. Remember: Events overwhelm plans.

14

Identify ways to make your story news today.

Remember, news is only news if it's new. Most shows are looking for a story that is hot today. A law professor at a local university began analyzing the O.J. Simpson trial on some of the constitutional issues, faxed his ideas to talk hosts and got himself on the air all over the country as an expert. This was quite an amazing feat for someone who would normally not have a newsworthy angle to get himself on the air. If you can't think of anything that makes your issue connect with what's hot, get some people in a room and brainstorm. Identify, identify, identify.

15

Come up with a catch phrase—something people will remember.

As President Clinton defended his position on affirmative action, he came up with the phrase "mend it, don't end it." Corny as it was, it was repeated by a ton of talk show hosts, and it stuck as a phrase that embodied his Administration's philosophy. The President is also widely quoted as talking about "those who work hard and play by the rules." Chuck Lewis of the Center for Public Integrity coined the term "Career Patrons" to describe groups, such as the National Rifle Association (NRA), that give out huge amounts of money through PACs. And who could forget the phrase from O.J. Simpson's trial, "If the glove doesn't fit, you must acquit."

See if you can paint pictures with your words, and show the conflicts where you can. "Compressed conflicts" is a concept developed by the Synectics folks in the sixties. They are two words that fight with each other, and put together they often form a great picture. These word images are the ones that will stay in peoples minds.

16

If you use statistics, be creative.

The sugar lobby knew that most people's eyes glaze when they hear about the cost of a pound of sugar. A few cents here or there isn't going to cause a storm of sympathy to members of Congress. But when those same statistics are put in a different context, such as national pride, it can change the energy behind your issue. The sugar lobby released some figures that show that U.S. consumers pay 28 percent less on purchases than consumers from other developed countries, and that Americans spend less on sugar as a percentage of income than any other country, with one exception. It didn't matter that the lobby was only looking out for its own interests. It translated the message to its advantage.

Another good way to use statistics is to mix them with stories. Give one statistic and then tell a story or anecdote to illustrate it. Be creative; come up with other indicators. If you want ideas, check the *Harper's Magazine* monthly index.

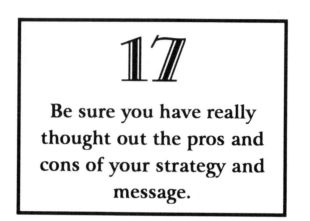

17

Be sure you have really thought out the pros and cons of your strategy and message.

Can you list the merits of each aspect of your strategy or message and the risks involved if you don't keep it? If you are knocking a person or organization, have you considered the negative political implications of this strategy? For example, Steve Forbes began a negative presidential campaign without considering the effect it would have on his own popularity; his ideas took hold with the Republicans, but he didn't.

18

Keep the public in mind when presenting your strategy.

If your issue is political, keep in mind that recent polls show 77 percent of Americans feel the federal government controls too much of our daily lives and 81 percent feel that government is wasteful. A *Times-*

Mirror survey reveals that callers to talk radio shows are the most extreme in anti-government sentiments. Before coming up with solutions that involve the government, remember these statistics. Acknowledge the general feeling, quote the statistics to show that you are at least aware of the general concerns of the population, then make your argument.

Keep the demographics of your target audience in mind. Will this radio campaign reach 30-year-old women driving BMWs in northeastern cities, or 55-year-old men driving trucks in the rural South? One radio host actually puts up a photograph in front of his microphone that illustrates his audience, so he has a visual reminder of who he is talking to.

Remember the basic cynicism of the American public at this stage in our history. A *Times-Mirror* survey showed that the greatest level of cynicism occurred between the ages of 30-39, followed by those in the 40-45 age group. In planning what you intend to say, allow for the basic level of cynicism.

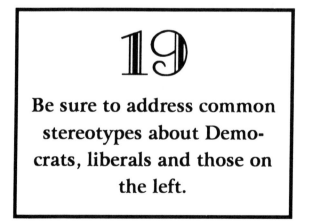

19

Be sure to address common stereotypes about Democrats, liberals and those on the left.

For example, overall perceptions of Democrats/Liberals and those on the left include:

- A Democrat is a Liberal. Similarly, liberals equate Republicans with conservatives.
- Liberals are in favor of big government and taxes.
- Democrats are nothing more than "tax and spend liberals."
- Liberals think that government is the solution to all problems.
- Democrats are anti-business and try to run everyone's life.
- Democrats support overregulation and are anti-business.
- Democrats and liberals are communists and believe that no one should own property.
- The left has no sense of humor.
- Liberals believe in sharing wealth instead of earning it.
- Most people on the left are the children of rich parents.

Be ready to confront how your issue dovetails with common stereotypes. Make a plan that includes addressing common assumptions in a way that is believable to the listening audience. Be able to give concrete examples. Make sure that your message appeals to people who work for a living. If you can afford it, it may be worth doing some focus group research. If not, do your own street research. Try making lists of new language and words that you want to use. Ask people in coffee shops, malls and grocery stores and so on what they think. How do your words sound to them? Do they hear and perceive any difference?

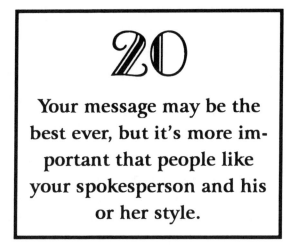

Think about a celebrity spokesperson that will get your issue on the air. Save the Children had a news conference right before the Women's Conference in Beijing. Normally, this would be a snooze and would not have drawn much press coverage but Sally Field held the news conference and press turned out in droves. Media, like everyone else, want to meet and be seen with stars. You don't even need a "hot" celebrity—a person with name-recognition will do the trick.

When President Clinton honored the 1996 Olympic athletes, all of the White House press attended with their children. Usually nothing phases the White House press corps. But they were like kids in a candy store waiting to meet the athletes and have photos taken with them.

It's important that people like your spokesperson. Consider how people respond to this individual when he or she walks into a room. Does he or she electrify the air or bring down the energy level? Either will come through on the air. One progressive group put someone on who sounded just like the annoying party guest everyone avoids. Although it was a great cause, no one wanted to listen to what the spokesperson was saying.

Radio requires more energy than television. Choose a spokesperson who conveys energy. Most radio programs avoid self-help authors like the plague. One self help author was able to get her book everywhere simply because she had lots of energy and was electric in her presentation of otherwise boring material. The spokesperson you choose is your best asset. Like any other asset, choose the person who speaks for you carefully. Several years ago, an enterprising psychiatrist Dr. Hugh Lurie, hired an actor to give a lecture to mental health professionals. He was told not to make logical sense. No one was told he was an actor. Everyone praised the lecture , saying it was one of the best lectures they had attended. Then Dr. Lurie replayed a video tape of the lecture to the same group. No one guessed the hoax. The moral of the story is that you can hold your audiences attention, even a very well educated audience's attention, if you can be entertaining. By the way, Dr. Lurie's tongue and cheek suggestion was to hire actors to teach medical school.

Help your spokesperson find the best tone for their personal style. Some folks are comfortable going on the offensive, but going on the offensive may not be the best solution for your personality. However, keep in mind the lawyer's adage: "When the facts are with you and the law is against you, pound the law. When the law is with you and the facts against you, pound the facts. When the law and facts are against you, pound the table."

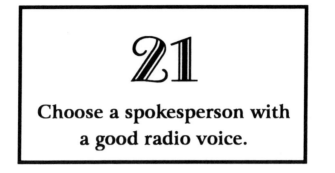

21

Choose a spokesperson with a good radio voice.

If you have a choice in a spokesperson, pay attention to how that person sounds over the air. Does he or she sound believable, at ease and professional? Record someone who you are considering and play the tape for people to get their reactions. Try not to use someone whose voice is grating, whiny or otherwise irritating.

Ed Asner, in discussing radio plays said: "The challenge of a radio play is to realize that you are there to excite the imagination of the listener. Everything you are trying to convey must be conveyed through your voice. No hand gestures, no winks, no blinks." Remember, talk radio is entertainment, especially while you are trying to convey information.

The spokesperson must be a good talker—articulate and quick-thinking—as well. The hosts rely on you to adequately prepare your speaker because in the world of media, perception is reality. As Aric Caplan says, "If your spokesperson comes across like a dud, they probably are. It's the difference between a Buick and a Corvette."

The spokesperson must be in sync with the background material you are sending out.

Can he or she back up what is in the material? It's important that he or she know it cold. Most hosts don't have time to read books or lengthy articles and rarely follow any issue as closely as an advocate does. Instead, they rely on the pitch material that is mailed or faxed to them. To keep the conversation going, your spokesperson must be able to carry it. It is wise to give your spokesperson a "source pack" that includes additional information on the topic to be covered.

Have your spokesperson listen to talk shows on a regular basis, particularly the day of or day before an interview.

By listening to the program, the spokesperson will know what issues are concerning people at the moment and may be able to anticipate some of the call-in questions. If your spokesperson is a politician or someone who cannot take time out of his day to listen, prepare a briefing memo about what is being discussed on the airwaves. Again, try to find a way to tie your issues to the hot topics.

24

Have some class.

It pays to do things with style and grace—people don't forget being treated well. A great example comes from the Republicans. A few days after the 1996 election Bob Dole wrote to Florida host Mark Sheinbaum. He apologized for not being able to grant him an interview before the election, but thanked him for interviewing some of the surrogate speakers. Definitely, a class response. A handwritten note to a host will always be appreciated.

When *Talkers Magazine* named the 100 Most Influential talk show hosts of the year, the House Republicans sprang into action. All of the 100 named hosts received a personal phone call from the head of the House Republican Conference as well as a congratulatory letter. There was absolutely no Democratic response.

4

Marketing a Campaign, Issue or Spokesperson

Be clever, have fun, develop games and giveaways.

Clever works, if it's appropriate. The Democratic National Committee gave its first Chicken Little Awards, replete with toy stuffed chickens, for the comments from Republicans that the sky would fall with the proposed budget. It was well conceived and made it on the evening news. A definite lighthearted one-two punch. An environmental group staged a 21-chain saw salute in front of the White House to protest logging. The sugar lobby sent out an all-day sucker to media outlets along with their pitch.

Develop games and giveaways to get your project noticed. During the long and arduous 1995 budget debate, Empower America developed a "Balance the Budget Game" in paper form and on the Internet. It made the point of the organization in a way that involved the public. What made it effective was that hosts could use the questions on the air and the organization was able to make their point by leading people to the answer on their own. A labor advocacy group brought bumper stickers that hosts could give away on the air. The stickers said, "The Labor Movement—the folks who brought you the weekend." Listeners loved it and the telephones rang off the hook.

Go ahead and do some wild things that will attract attention. Send out great cartoons, those that make you laugh about your issue. When they were trying to make their case for females-only wait staff, Hooters had people with frisbees flying all over Washington with photos of a male waiter dressed in drag. Everyone wanted one, staffers from Capitol hill were leaving their offices in pursuit of a free Hooters frisbee. It made for great P.R., and somehow the Equal Employment Opportunity Commission lost its intense interest in the Hooters case. Haley Barber, Chairman of the Republican National Committee, had an ad issuing a million-dollar challenge to anyone who could prove they were cutting Medicare spending. Everyone on talk radio talked about the ad. Right or wrong with the facts, it made for great talk. The Democrats filled their actuality line with Democratic-oriented Christmas carols. After all, if you have fun with your pitch and campaign so will the people who are the intended recipients.

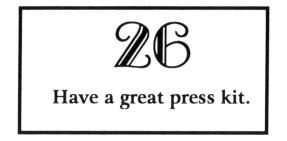

26

Have a great press kit.

A good press kit is essential. It acts as an introduction to the material you are presenting. Your pitch should appear on the outside of the kit. The "must have" elements are: an up-to-date press release (write new ones or change the date and some of the questions on old ones because no one likes old news), a good, recent bio of your spokesperson or persons, a set of suggested questions for the guest that are not too heavily weighted toward your position (everyone wants to have a spokesperson that is familiar with all sides of an argument), and the position paper on your organization or issue. Put these in the form of bullets and quick headers that the producer can use to promote the issue and the spokesperson. Consider re-faxing updated talking points on the day of an interview.

Make sure your materials look professional. It's great to have a press kit in a nice shiny folder but it can be very expensive and not necessary. What is important, however, is that it looks and feels like a professional job. It is better to send out two pages of succinct professional looking material than a shiny folder hastily put together with poorly printed documents.

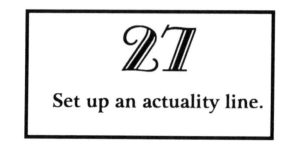

27

Set up an actuality line.

Actuality lines are a great way to become more customer service oriented. An actuality is a short sound bite that helps promote your message in a way that enhances an on-air news story. They can help you get on radio stations all over the country. They are a good way to saturate a market because if they are used, they are rebroadcast several times a day.

There is special equipment available that makes it possible to set up a phone line "on the cheap" with a simple voice mail system that people can phone to retrieve your actuality. Be sure to choose a method of delivery that gives good sound quality, however, so stations can air it. The phone companies now offer voice mail that can support broadcast quality sound. In general, talk shows do not use actualities so this should be directed to the news departments of every radio station you can find.

Relate actualities to news or they won't get used. If you are sending out a press release, quote the head of your organization, etc. and record them saying it for your line. Be sure to note on the release that sound is available. If you have staged an event or someone from your organization is giving a speech, take a sound bite directly from that. It's always better than the "canned" quote because it makes it seem as though the radio station's reporter was there.

Some pointers in using actualities are:

- Keep the actualities short (a maximum of 10-20 seconds).
- Have your line attached to a toll-free 800 or 888 number. It's not very expensive for you and will significantly increase the number of stations who will call.
- Conversely, it is not essential to have an 800 number. There are very successful actuality lines that aren't toll-free. They succeed because they provide producers with good quality and room for editorial decision-making.
- Make sure the quality is consistently good. If you put bad quality actualities out a few times, news directors will quit calling.
- Don't offer actualities just to offer actualities. If you put up actualities that have no news value and just spew rhetoric, no one will use them and no one will take you seriously.
- Make sure that you put each actuality on twice so that stations can set levels on the first and record on the second.

- Fax, phone or e-mail stations to let them know what is available and what will be coming up. Make sure you provide them with the total time of each actuality. Just like interviews, actualities need to be advertised. Make sure that you "pitch" before your feed, so that you get maximum exposure.

- If your spokesperson speaks another language, such as Spanish, put your actuality up in that language as well. Pitch to Spanish language stations.

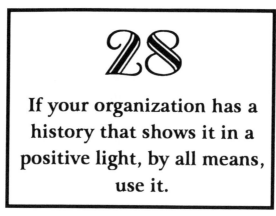

28

If your organization has a history that shows it in a positive light, by all means, use it.

In the never-ending search for relevant ways to bring up your issue, don't forget your organization's history. Think about creative and timely ways to highlight your credentials. A great example is that during the Anniversary of Women's Suffrage the Republicans sent out massive amounts of publicity about how the Twenty-First Amendment was introduced by a Republican. Most people were completely unaware that it was the Republicans who had promoted women's suffrage.

Be sure you always have the mission statement of your organization available. Use it !

29

Do something fun and do it regularly.

The Progressive Caucus in Congress came up with a "Gilded Lily" award, for the group that benefitted the most from Congressional corporate welfare. Republican Congressman Joel Hefley began a "Porker of the Week" award. He is heard all over the country on radio stations. He has made a name for himself, and most importantly, he is willing to get on the air outside of his Congressional district.

People begin to anticipate something on a monthly basis (radio stations come to expect it) and it sets up a way that you can make a regular headline and radio booking. In a twist on this technique, Senator Lieberman makes it a habit to have breakfast at local diners with constituents. The media doesn't always show up to cover these breakfasts, but when they do, it's terrific press. And even if the media doesn't show up, these breakfasts still show the Senator to be a real person.

30

Create events that stations and hosts will want to cover.

Invite stations and hosts to cover a big event. Be prepared to pay for the lines (telephone and ISDN) so that stations and hosts will be able to broadcast. The Democratic Leadership Council got a mountain of free press by inviting talk hosts to broadcast from their conference. They made it simple by polling the stations and hosts as to what kind of equipment was needed, times they wanted to broadcast and making sure that hosts and producers were allowed into the invitation only events. All guests, including many Senators and members of Congress, were available for interviews. It was a class operation and won kudos from the hosts. The Democratic Leadership Council was smart enough to contact the National Association of Radio Talk Show Hosts (NARTSH) and didn't just invite Democrat-friendly hosts.

Republicans in Congress took advantage of the first one hundred days of their leadership by inviting hosts to broadcast from the Capitol. Hosts responded but a repeat was not as successful. Why? Because the cost of installing the lines was borne by the stations. It proved too expensive for stations to do more than once a year.

You can have a great event, but if you don't handle the press well you will have wasted a lot of effort. During the 1996 Democratic National Convention, the former Chicago Seven held a concert, rally and press conference. It could have been a great media event. But, press was not well planned. Media was told they would get interviews , and it turned out to be a free for all, with press having to grab time with the various personalities. Plus, noise made it impossible to get good radio interviews. One of the sponsors of the event, *The Nation,* gave up on site press responsibility to another group, and many press folks went away unhappy. Moral of the story: Plan ahead and if you are sponsoring an event, know who is going to be there, pitch the people you want to be there, and make sure that you don't abdicate responsibility. Have a separate room for radio interviews. Make a schedule of one-on-one interviews and stick to it. It is your organization's or candidate's name on the event. Treat it as you would the family jewels.

31

Send real information in addition to your press kit material.

Send relevant newspaper and magazine articles to hosts and producers before and after your program.

This falls into the category of making the hosts' and producers' jobs easier. Most producers and hosts, if they are good at their craft, will do their own research and will have a pretty good sense of what the opposition is saying, but it is still helpful to provide them with material that relates to the other side. Then, of course, be ready to make mincemeat of the arguments. Graphs, charts, sources and statistics are always welcome for the producer. Visuals, obviously, won't work for the interview.

Make talk show folks think that you're including them and not just sending them your regular press releases. Again, you've got to hand it to the Republicans. They send out the same talking points to the radio hosts that they send to the political troops. They also send a regular memo written for "Republican Leaders" to hosts. This is terrific, because hosts don't want to feel that they are always being "spun." Many hosts will continue to discuss an issue days or weeks after you have been on the air, so be sure you keep them informed.

Don't send so much material that you give away your punch line. While you want to send good information, you want it to also be enticing so that a producer is prompted to want your spokesperson to come on air and "fill in the blanks."

Put your talking points on a card, and send the card out.

This is a great way to make your point a little different, and to have it easy and accessible for the host to read. Any printer can accommodate you. You can date them and offer them as a set. (This is also useful for politicians and their staff members.)

Provide a planning calendar.

The Republicans are masters of this. They send around a calendar on a weekly basis, listing events several months in advance. It helps producers and because the dates are repeated, it helps ensure that they will be remembered. It's especially good for chaotic, paper-filled offices where things get buried. You can't rely on the local daybook. People can accommodate you best when you make it into their planning calendar. Stations strive to cover news and therefore want to anticipate events; a calendar can help them do so.

34

Find out something about your host/station and area.

This can be tough to do if you are attempting a nationwide media blitz, but it will help get you on the air and keep you there longer. As Tip O'Neill said, "All politics is local." The more you're able to localize an issue with specific examples, the more you will be able to get your message across to listeners. Mention how decisions are made locally, how your organization uses the local community and members to steer organizational direction. Have your staff/organization take some time to find out some basics about the area or host and use that in your discussion. A good place to start may be calling the local Chamber of Commerce or running an on-line computer search on the town/city and local newspapers to find out what issues are hot in the area. If you represent a national organization or branch of government, call like organizations/government agencies to get a sense of the local mind set. Remember, hosts, like teachers, have eyes in the backs of their heads, and their ears to the ground in their community. Do not call around locally to find out "the political spin" of the host; they may find out and it will annoy them. If you must call somebody local, call the media critic at the local paper. They know talk stations and are often happy to give you the score.

35

Use a book or booklet for publicity.

If you don't already have one, consider writing a small book, booklet or pamphlet before you begin your on-air campaign. It's amazing what a little hand out can do to promote legitimacy and interest in your cause. The Center for Constitutional Rights in New York City has a booklet, "When the Agent Knocks." Although the Center is often dismissed by hosts as one of those "left wing organizations," the booklet gets interest in these days of paranoia about government.

36

To make sure that your issue is heard on the air, train some of your folks to listen to talk radio and to call in.

There are tons of folks willing to do this: parents who are home with small children, people with a day off, people commuting who have access to car phones and students or other volunteers. Having a cadre of people call in regularly does several things. It make sure the airwaves are exposed to your issue and that it gets mentioned on radio. It can engage the host and other audience into legitimate conversation, and if the host perceives interest in your topic, it can make it easier to book your spokesperson. In addition to calling, these folks can also fax the radio shows with letters about your issue. Again, the idea is to keep your issue on the front burner. In hot campaigns, remember that for every minute one of your people are on the radio, the other side isn't on. Even if your callers are not great at radio, at least it is your point of view, not the oppositions. During the 1996 elections, Brooke Stroud, working for the Democratic National Committee had regular conference calls with women in the party. The calls were designed to get women to call in to talk shows, discuss the elections and encourage women to vote. All the women with whom Brooke was working, from all over the state, participated .

When you are training the troops to make calls- give them the following tips:

- Keep a list of talk programs, times and stations along with numbers. This way they can find out where and who to listen to. Remember the Internet. There are lot's of programs to listen to and call into. If you have a TVRO (satellite dish) many syndicated programs are heard there as well, and most programs love satellite call ins.

- Very popular programs will require a wait. Call in at the top of the hour and during breaks. Many hosts love to talk even if they have callers backed up. Be prepared to wait.

- If a station is trying to reach a younger demographic, then they might screen out older sounding calls. Same thing goes for women, etc. You may want to arrange to have your call made by those who fit the demographic that the station is aiming for.

- Relate your personal experience to the topic. If they are discussing education , a teacher is a great person to call. If parenting is the topic, there is no better expert than a parent.

- Address the host by name. Make sure they know that you are listening to them. Do not call a show you are not listening to. Producers and call screeners are wise to such tricks.

- Many local and national shows have caller ID. Don't try to change voices, or say you are from a different location. They will wipe you off the show forever.

- Make sure that once your call is answered that you turn off the radio. There is a delay. You can then listen on the telephone.

- If you are a first time caller say so. Hosts love first time callers. Say something complimentary about the show, if you can be genuine about it. You don't have to agree. You can say "I have a different perspective, but I find your show informative and entertaining." Just don't be phony or sound phony.

- To get the other side in an argument to really hear what you are saying, repeat what you agree with, but say it quickly. Work at what you are going to say, write it down and then shorten it.

- If you are going to ask a question, then ask it. Don't say "I want to ask a question" and then go into a long monologue. Ask your question or make a statement.

- If you have backup for what you are saying, such as a book or statistic, use it. If you saw something on television or heard it somewhere else, be sure to be specific about it. The host and audience will be grateful. Be careful however when you are mentioning another radio station's call letters, it will not make the host happy.

- Remember, this is a conversation. It is not a sermon and it is not a chance to read on the air. Let professionals read, and callers engage in conversation.

- People on the "outs" often make the best callers. The standard party line gets boring.

- Don't be offended if the host is abrupt with you. They are there to keep ratings up and entertain the audience, not to establish friendships.

- Turn off your call waiting. It sounds awful on the air.

- Kids, animals, and background television, or music will distract you and the listeners. Go to a place where you will not be distracted. On the other hand, hosts love it when you are driving in your car and get enthused when you tell them that something on their show made you pull off the road.

- Be sure and tell the producer/screener that you are on a car phone if you are one. They will often put you at the head of the line.

- Don't insult the host. It's not the politic thing to do.

- Remember a rule of assertiveness training—You can be a bit of broken record, repeating your point (but not too much) and not backing off. If the host tries to throw you off guard, stick to your point.

- No one can argue with how you feel. Remember a feeling is not a fact and it represents what you really believe. When you use personal examples, it is hard to argue with your experience. Other callers will agree with you more if they can like you and identify with your situation. Without being Pollyanna, be someone that other callers can see living next door to them.

- Never lie to the screener to get on the air. You can say how you have a different viewpoint. Many hosts will throw someone off immediately if they suspect they have been lied to.

Get an 800 or 888 number.

Spend a few extra bucks and invest in an 800 or 888 number. It is amazing how many times a host will ask a guest if he or she has an 800 or an 888 number, and either the spokesperson doesn't have one or he or she doesn't remember it. Have a number the public can call and ask the host if you can give it out. Give the hours of operation. Make sure there is someone to give written or oral information when listeners call. You might also want to consider a "fax on demand" service that allows listeners to call and request relevant information to be faxed back to them.

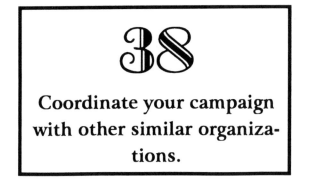

38

Coordinate your campaign with other similar organizations.

It is impossible to ignore an issue when it is brought up again and again, especially if it is presented in different ways with different spokespersons. If your issue is the federal budget (a very dry issue) you are going to want to coordinate with other groups who support your stance and can cover the specific areas in a way that is relevant to the listeners. Let listeners know you are working with like-minded groups. Let them know you are sharing information and resources. Competition should only exist between opposing groups, so working together with groups on your side is a great idea.

Be willing to debate.

You may be able to get your side of an argument on the air with greater ease if you set up a debate and offer it as a package to stations. Of course, this might mean dialogue with the enemy, but it might astronomically increase your chances of getting your issues publicized. You may need to work with an intermediary not associated with either organization to get it going. Remember, it is better an issue be debated than not be heard at all. In fact, you can't have a credible discussion of an issue if it's obviously one-sided.

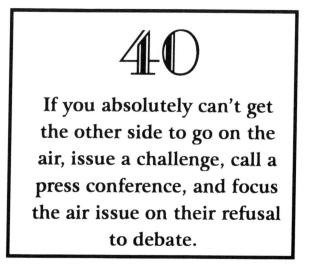

If you absolutely can't get the other side to go on the air, issue a challenge, call a press conference, and focus the air issue on their refusal to debate.

If all else fails and the other side will not debate you, you can issue a challenge in print and on the air and force them to debate you. Radio folks hate cowards, and if the other side won't debate you, people want to know about it. Make sure that you save all the documentation and correspondence of this challenge. You could make political hay out of the opposition's refusal to debate. When Florida sugar farmers refused to debate Nat Reed, a south Florida conservationist, he brought an empty chair to the studio and referred to it throughout the interview.

Like with all press conferences , make sure you have something interesting to shoot, in case you are able to get television there. Of course, a press conference on the steps of your opponents office always makes for an interesting photo op, especially if there are some banners in the background.

5

Booking A Spokesperson

41

**Be willing to book all kinds
of shows and formats.**

See what you can do to get your issue on different
kinds of formats. Radio news uses short stories with
quick interviews and provides a lot of bang for the buck
because they repeat the segment several times during
the day or over a weekend. Christian stations are often
overlooked by progressive organizations: They are

often a rich source of good interview possibilities. Ethnic stations, sports stations and specialty stations, as well as weekend talk programs are great sources of interviews and are often overlooked. Morning zoos are light, funny and very topical, and they have huge audiences. Be equally as willing to accept a five minute interview as you would an hour long one.

Don't forget weekend and late night programs too. Most people think about booking on daily Monday through Friday programs. The second most listened to time is between 10 a.m. and 3 p.m. on Saturdays. There is a wealth of programming on weekends. It's a great time to get your issue heard. Remember, lots of people are in their cars on weekends, often with family members, so it's important to orient your presentation with a family audience in mind. Art Bell and Stan Major, two currently popular overnight hosts, have a ton of listeners. Set your alarm clock and be ready to talk.

Be willing to book conservative talk shows but watch out for the crazies. Some radio hosts will use attack radio which means they will find anything in your organization's background or spokesperson that may be embarrassing. (Read some of Howard Stern's *Miss America* if you don't understand attack radio— although he is far from crazy.) Unless you're squeaky clean, be prepared to make some good, strong comebacks. It should be noted, however, that most conservative hosts are not attack radio hosts and that even an attack host can be worth your while if you have a sense of humor and can roll with the punches. Just make sure you and your organization don't have skeletons in your closet or if you do, your spokesperson is prepared to answer questions about them.

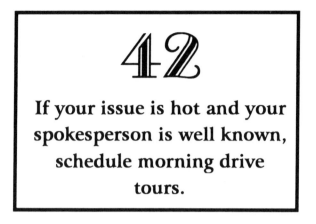

42

If your issue is hot and your spokesperson is well known, schedule morning drive tours.

Your booking department or scheduler should identify 50 to 60 markets and national shows in which you are interested and then pitch to each station individually. Offer three to ten minute interviews. Schedule the first interview at 6:30 or 7:00 a.m. and map out a schedule of about 20 to 25 stations with three to five stations per hour. You can use this strategy to cover a good portion of the United States and millions of listeners or you can downsize it for a regional or statewide campaign.

You will need:

- Two telephone lines in two rooms;
- An assistant to make the calls to connect your spokesperson to each station;
- A few newspapers (probably from different regions of the country) so that the spokesperson can relate to the news of the day. Access to

Reuters, Associated Press and the PR Newswire would also be very helpful; and

• Food to keep your spokesperson going for six hours.

Note: Drive time tours are difficult to arrange so that you get the best stations and programs. You may want to contract out a good P.R. firm who does this kind of work. As with surgeons and open heart surgery, success in a drive time tour has a lot to do with how frequently the P.R. firm does them. Choose firms that know radio and regularly deal with hosts and producers to do this work. It might also be useful to find a local station or agency that will let you use their ISDN line. It makes it sound as if you are actually in the studio.

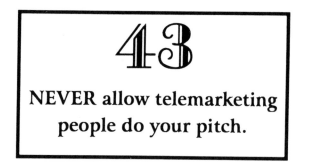

43

NEVER allow telemarketing people do your pitch.

A producer's job is to spend the day on the telephone. The last thing he or she wants is a mechanized conversation with someone who knows nothing about radio and is just reading from a script. It loses the one thing that makes all the difference when it comes to booking guests for a radio talk show: the personal relationship with the producers and the host. The person making the pitch must be knowledgeable. At minimum, he or she should have a biography or resume so that if a producer asks questions, they can be easily answered.

44

The phone call is just the first step in your pitch.

Like another customer service provider, you are offering a product or service. Your job is to be of service to your customer (producer/host of the program). This involves establishing a relationship with him or her so you can be called on as a resource for guests or information. For example, if a producer isn't interested in a guest, offer an actuality. (Don't use the word sound bite for actuality.) The producer says there's no room for that? Offer some information on the issue along side of what the other side is saying. Ask, if he or she wants more background material. How did this issue fare in Congress in the past? What local people have taken up the cause? How has this affected the local area? All of these topics may interest the host/producer.

Remember, you are interrupting producers' extremely busy days. One way to avoid making yourself a pest is to begin a call with an apology. "I'm really sorry to bother you, can I just have a few seconds of your time?" Be a little self-deprecating: "I know you're very busy, but I've really got to get my spokesperson on the air." Let them understand that you have a job to do, just like they do.

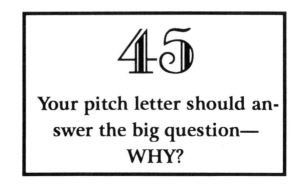

45

Your pitch letter should answer the big question— WHY?

Why this issue? Why this issue now? Why this particular spokesperson? Why is this issue more important than __ ? Why is booking this guest or issue going to make an impact on the audience? When preparing your letter, use the "who cares" test: ask yourself who cares about your issue and why anyone should care.

46

Faxes don't have voices.

Yes, by all means send a fax with your proposed program, spokesperson and hot issue, but don't rely on it to get you the interview. You need a person to follow-up. Often, you can make your case better personally than with a piece of paper. You may also really connect with the producer in person.

Be sure to offer to send the fax again. Often it gets overlooked. It may have been written in a way that did not get noticed. The balanced budget people sent a simple fax every day, with the number of days without a balanced budget. Its simplicity stood out and certainly made the point. Faxes do work, especially with good follow-up.

47

Consider conference calls with several hosts or news stations.

If you have limited time with your spokesperson or you want to get an issue on the air in a crisis situation, consider the conference call. This will allow you to speak with several news stations and talk hosts at the same time. There are several ways to do it. The best strategy is to have your spokesperson available to answer questions which stations can record. Sometimes, you may want to provide a spokesperson for "background" (something that will not be on the air). This is somewhat dangerous, as news people are used to it, but talk radio people don't generally like to be involved in something they can't quote or use directly on the air. During the budget crisis, Americans for Tax

Reform arranged a daily update on the budget, with a different person from the Congressional leadership each day. The calls were very effective and provided smaller stations with access that they could not otherwise have.

Note: If any of the stations are in the same geographic area, they might object to the conference call format.

Another Note: If you are going to have print reporters on the call, remind them that keystrokes on the computer will ruin the recording for stations taping the call. Ask them to mute their phones while typing.

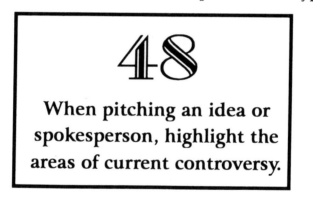

48

When pitching an idea or spokesperson, highlight the areas of current controversy.

On first glance, pornography on the Internet seemed like something everyone could agree on. But, when enforcement issues are brought up, the issue became a hot topic of conversation. Make sure the areas of controversy are clearly stated in your pitch literature so that they are immediately obvious.

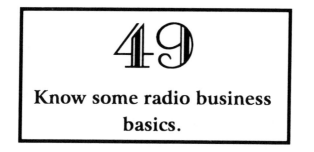

49

Know some radio business basics.

Adjust to news and talk hours. Larger stations with a news or talk format may have certain producers that work only after 8:00 p.m.. Be sure to do some of your pitching to them and, of course, provide your pager number. In the news format, much of what gets on the air for morning drive gets put on during the wee hours of the morning. If you live in the same city as the late night folks, send over doughnuts or cookies as a thank-you. Most P.R. folks forget about the evening and late shift in radio. If you have an evening or night host's home phone number don't use it much before 3:00 p.m. because he or she is probably sleeping.

Talk shows work daily to increase "time spent listening on the air" and "new listeners." Keep those twin goals in mind as you make your pitch. Unless you know that a station's demographics is older, aim your message at the population between the ages of 25 and 54 because that's the group that interests sponsors and programmers the most. Although an older demographic also listens to talk radio, sponsors consider the older demographic death to business. It isn't correct, but that's the perception.

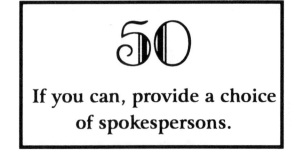

If you can, provide a choice of spokespersons.

A written list is worth its weight in gold. Many stations have databases and if they can't use your spokesperson now, they may be able to do so later. Put together a short bio on each person that makes them human. Often there may be one detail that catches a producer's eye.

If your group is large, publish a guide to possible guest "experts." Send it to potential hosts.

Offering two choices at the time of the pitch can be effective. As an example, you can suggest the Executive Director of an agency who could speak intelligently about a broad range of issues related to your central issue. In addition, you could offer to book someone who can tell a compelling personal story that relates to your issue. So, if AIDS is your issue, you could make two suggestions. One might be the director a local AIDS service organization who knows about many service delivery issues. The other might be a person living with AIDS who can talk in real terms about what it's like to live with the disease on a daily basis.

51

If you must cancel, offer to provide a substitute.

Don't leave a producer in the lurch. Many shows promote guests on-air or in the newspapers prior to the interview. If you have to cancel, try to provide another guest who is as close to an equivalent as you can come. Always offer to rebook. If it was a big name guest and they have to cancel, sending a plant or a box of candy as well as a note goes a long way. Senator Kennedy was scheduled to do a show with actress Whoopi Goldberg. At the last minute Ms. Goldberg was called to the White House. Senator Kennedy apologized on the air and offered on the air to help the host rebook Ms. Goldberg. This helped with the host's promotion problem and showed the Senator was sincere.

If you mess up, apologize in writing immediately. A congressional leader was booked on several talk shows over a three-week period. At the last minute he canceled several shows. No apology or viable explanation was given. Unfortunately for the politician, several hosts were together at a national forum, exchanging war stories, they compared notes and found they had all been stiffed by the same politician. The hosts are still waiting for a letter of explanation, and those hosts have vowed not to extend an invitation again to the politician.

6

Cultivating Relationships With Producers And Hosts

52

Spend time with the press.

Invite press members to social gatherings and your events. It can be very helpful to treat press well and that includes news directors, assignment editors, reporters, hosts and producers. There's a saying among press in Washington, "You'll eat at Republican events, but be sure to go to Democratic events with your stomach full." Believe it or not, Republicans let press eat at their events. In general, Democrats do not. There is no substitute for good old-fashioned hospitality. It's a great time to get people to know you and it will help make you and your organization remembered. Consider having an event for the media. If you can't afford to stage an event on an annual or semiannual basis, consider staging an event with other like-minded organizations.

Become part of the radio community. Read *Talkers Magazine*. Attend conventions such as the National Association of Radio Talk Show Hosts, The Radio and TV News Directors Association, and the National Association of Broadcasters' Radio Convention. Some of the big guys such as Rush Limbaugh and Don Imus don't attend, but lots of influential hosts, producers and program directors do. You'll get to meet people and make social contacts. It's important not to try to line up interviews at these events because establishing a relationship first is more important. Industry people don't go to these things to be badgered. They go to let their hair down.

Make reference to the host when you can. The media loves to read or hear about itself. Refer to shows or stories that you know about the host and the radio stations activities. Tell stories that you know involve the host and their interests.

Be sensitive to the host's needs.

The producers and hosts are your customers. You are getting free publicity. Doug Stephan says, "If you ever doubt the value of what you are getting, call up the station or network for their ad rates." You are getting the value of those 60 second ads times the number of minutes you are on the air. Remember this in your attitude toward the producer and the host. They are your customers and should be treated accordingly.

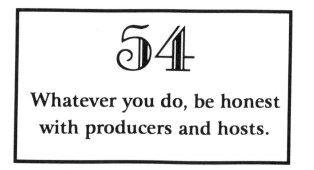

Whatever you do, be honest with producers and hosts.

Radio folks know each other and they talk. If you decide to "upgrade" the station or network on which your guest is to be booked on, don't lie to a producer. Someone from that network or station will be talking to someone, or traveling through a city and hear your guest. This recently happened during a major book tour. The publicist was less than honest and in the long run, it created hard feelings toward the publisher.

Use care when granting first dibs or exclusivity to radio stations. First, be sure you are doing this with the best station for your needs. Then, be sure to be very clear with the station that you are granting exclusivity.

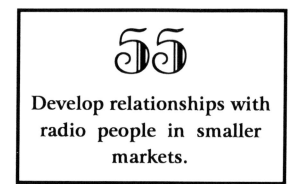

55

Develop relationships with radio people in smaller markets.

Plan for the long haul, as well as the short term. The Cleveland Indians made it to the World Series in 1995 after having been out of it for forty-two years. They did it by developing over a five-year period strong farm teams and bringing up young players. Like professional athletes, radio people move around and move up. Find hosts and news people that you can work within smaller markets and develop a relationship with them. They will bask in the attention and remember you and your issue throughout their career.

56

Don't drive producers crazy asking for stuff.

If you want a tape of your in-studio interview, furnish your own tape prior to the interview. If you want a tape of a phone interview, send a tape and a return postage paid envelope before the interview. Of course you want to hear yourself on the radio, or have Aunt Selma hear you, but if it creates extra work for the producer or host, it will generally be annoying. A producer's job is to put on a show, not take care of your needs.

Many networks treat their station lists as proprietary and they don't let them out. Producers don't always have access to station coverage maps. You can make a polite inquiry, but don't bug them.

57

Don't ever ask about the political beliefs of a press person—It will always get you in trouble.

Radio people take the First Amendment—freedom of the press—dead seriously. Don't do anything that even appears to threaten that.

Energy Secretary Hazel O'Leary made the mistake of hiring a firm to rate press coverage. Someone leaked the document, and it made great talk on talk shows.

A talk show host left an abortion rights organization's press conference after talking with the press person and requesting a guest for her show. The press person immediately placed a call to the host's station to ask if she was of the same political persuasion as Rush Limbaugh. The host was actually pro-choice, but advocacy groups considered what she did to be "spying." What ever you call it, the technique created great over-the-air discussion on the host's program.

It's okay to ask how a host or producer got into the business as an icebreaker if you're visiting the station. Otherwise, steer clear of personal questions.

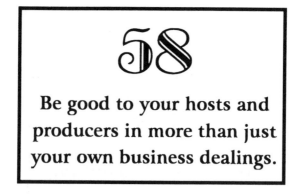

58

Be good to your hosts and producers in more than just your own business dealings.

For example, if there is a producer of a smaller show who you know wants to move on and you feel good about recommending this person to friends, do so. Don't assume that if he or she is gone, so is your contact. You can build a relationship with a new producer and you'll have a friend for life in the one you helped. That's how you build up your network. The ultimate benefit might just be that a producer refers you or your spokesperson to a colleague for a show.

When radio stations or other media do something right or put on a good show or guest, let them know. Make sure others let them know. Radio stations react to mail and will put your letter in the "public file." It encourages them to do "right" in the future.

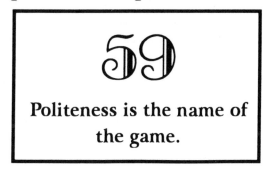

59

Politeness is the name of the game.

If you try to book guests and fail a few times, but are very polite, the producer will admire your persistence and appreciate your politeness. You will most likely get a booking eventually. For example, a host had met a woman at a party. They talked about her issue and the host suggested they might do a show. Later, the woman called and left a terse message saying, "I hope you'll honor your commitment to do a show." The host felt the woman was demanding and nasty and never called her back. This is not a great way to get on a show.

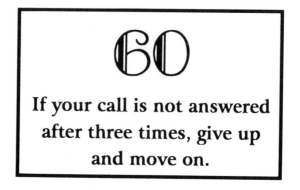

60

If your call is not answered after three times, give up and move on.

You don't want to alienate producers and hosts because you might need them again. However, if the producer has said he has to talk to the host, you can be a bit more persistent. Radio talk show hosts have more say than television hosts. Often the host makes the final decision. If you don't get an out and out no, then it is worth pursuing. Ask the producer if there is anything else you can provide to help with a decision. You can always back to a producer with a timely idea.

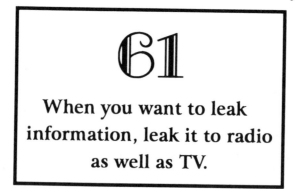

61

When you want to leak information, leak it to radio as well as TV.

It is quite amazing that many politicians choose to leak to a newspaper, or sometimes a TV station, but forget about the power of the radio and its captive driving audience. When you want to leak something, don't forget radio. Radio folks appreciate the heads up, and you may get more coverage than from the newspaper. You certainly will get a different audience. Radio also allows you to target your audience much more effectively than newspapers or television and that can be especially helpful in cases such as these. Keep in mind that radio stations are often owned by conglomerates and might have sister stations that should also receive the information.

A few years back, Jay Byrne worked on the congressional campaign of Mike Kopetski. He had folks calling up talk shows and relating stories to whatever the host was discussing. If the host was talking about scenic bridges, he had people calling about infrastructure. He also got around the local procedure that some newspapers often did not want to publish articles about radio programs by making transcripts and then writing about what had been discussed on a specific program. He would send out press releases stating that "It's just not Denny's week." Soon newspapers picked up the expression. Radio, if used properly, can give you entré to other media. Think of talk radio first, not last, when planning your campaign.

Make your spokespersons available to stations and hosts off the air as well as on the air.

Your research department should be willing to help news departments, hosts and producers find answers to their questions. When a radio show calls, it's best to "share the wealth" and not be proprietary with information. The main point here is to be viewed as a helpful resource for stations, hosts and producers. If you can, share opposition research with producers. You will have friends for life and may get tips in exchange.

Offering information that makes the news department or host look good will buy you loyalty and also allows you to get information on the air without needing to book a spokesperson. If you give good, reliable information, it will help you gain credibility for your issue and spokesperson.

Always send written confirmation by fax or e-mail for your booking.

Follow it up with a phone call. Be sure to include your back up and pager numbers in case you forget the booking. Everyone will be happier, it's more professional and prevents verbal miscommunication. Keep a copy in your booking file.

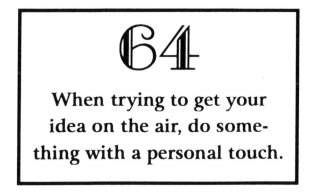

When trying to get your idea on the air, do something with a personal touch.

Learn the names of news directors and program managers, so you can address letters and phone calls to them directly. If you know your host or producer is interested in something special, send them an article or book. If you can afford to, send it by messenger (if you are in the same city). It will make producers and hosts think that you are taking the time to meet their needs (and with luck that will translate into the producer and host meeting your needs in the future).

7

Being an Effective Spokesperson

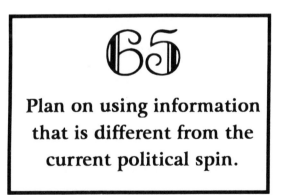

65

Plan on using information
that is different from the
current political spin.

Talk show hosts who have interviewed many people
from the same political party on the same issues often
feel that the voices change but the words remain the
same. Listeners will be bored hearing the same political
spin. If you are speaking on a popular political issue,

listen to what everyone else is saying and say something different. Tell a funny story or give a human example. People will respect and take notice of a refreshing true view of the facts and numbers rather than the same old spin.

Weigh the scale of predictability and the value of repetition with the boredom factor. Give your standard stump speech a definite date. President Clinton came up in the polls with his speech on "Common Ground." Many Americans could relate to it, but just as it was getting too predictable, the President switched from his familiar phrase to new ones. That's the secret of being able to get your issue heard over time; make sure your material is fresh and not overused.

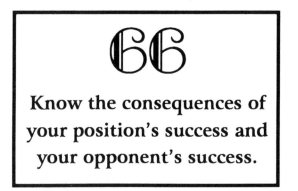

66

Know the consequences of your position's success and your opponent's success.

Be able to articulate what would happen if your position on an issue became policy. Similarly, be ready to speak about the likely consequences if the opposite position won the day. Lay out the issue in concrete terms. The average American couldn't give two hoots about a spotted owl when they see people out of work because of them. As a result, the spotted owl became a talk show mantra. Environmentalists could have couched their position in a number of appealing ways.

Eventual jobs, re-creating the environment, the importance of National Parks, alternative ways of harvesting forest, lifesaving drugs, renewable natural resources and positive effects on the economy mean much more to listeners.

Similarly, be able to explain clearly what you think will happen if your opponent's strategy is implemented. Democrats lost some real ground on the welfare/food stamps battle by the doom strategy. Most listeners had a hard time understanding the idea of cuts when there was more money in the budget. Inflation and the rate of increase of health care costs were lost on an audience that saw more money in the bottom line. What hit home more were increased out-of-pocket Medicare premium expenses. Those guests who were able to give specific examples of what changing nursing home regulations might mean to family members and to the aging baby boomers were able to score with the listeners. The more specific and concrete the example, the better chance of making a home run. In a debate situation, allow the opposition to talk themselves into a corner with their misinformation and half-truths and then respond concisely with the correct information.

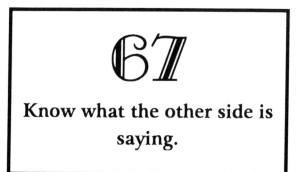

67

Know what the other side is saying.

Do whatever you can to know exactly what arguments your opponents are using. Read the papers, listen to their interviews, attend their lectures and speeches and read everything they are writing. Listen with a group of people outside your organization if you can. Find out what people like about what the competition is saying, what really grabs them and makes them pay attention.

Activist Jeanette Fruen recommends keeping a clipping file with copies of every article and editorial on all sides of your issue, noting the newspaper, page and date of the article. She also recommends keeping these clips in chronological order. This may show biased coverage or a change in views. Fruen used her files extensively and effectively in the Senator Packwood sexual harassment case.

68

Be prepared to deal with credibility issues.

Credibility is always a problem if you, or your organization, is not well known. Therefore, you must be ready to bolster listeners' belief in your credibility. To enhance the credibility of your spokesperson, list speaking engagements and broadcast programs he or she has been on. Be sure to provide recent, positive examples of what has been promised and then accomplished, providing concrete examples and references.

Deal appropriately with any skeletons in your closet. Perhaps your organization is in a credibility slump because of some recent scandal or troublesome history. In that case, it is essential that you be ready to address the issue simply and non-defensively. Then, move beyond the issue by focusing on current activities.

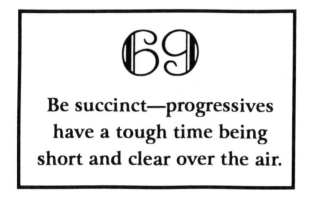

69

Be succinct—progressives have a tough time being short and clear over the air.

There's a saying, "it takes more time to write a short letter then a long one." Craft your words ahead of time, as if you are writing an article, but then memorize the main points. Remember how much you liked those teachers in college, the ones who told a joke, didn't take themselves too seriously and were well prepared. It's the same way on radio.

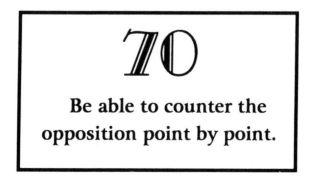

70

Be able to counter the opposition point by point.

Make a handout that puts their argument on one side of the page and yours on the other. If you can reinforce your argument, all the better. Make your "Point by Point" available to your host and his or her producer. It's also a great giveaway that you can offer by 800 number, fax on demand or Internet. Remember, never knock a person, only their behavior or ideology. You're in the business of winning people over to your side, not burning bridges. As stated earlier: research the opposition. There is no replacement!

71

Use the Rule of Three to assess on-air performance.

The Rule of Three is a handy guide that anyone can use to judge the impact of what is said on the air. Michael Albl, Executive Vice President of Marketing from Critical Mass Media explains that you can ask the following three questions to determine whether an item or piece used on the air is funny, compelling, interesting, informative—or any other adjective you care to insert into the questions. For example, using the word "funny" in the Rule of Three, the questions to ask are:

1. Is (or was) the element funny?

2. Is (or was) the element real funny?

3. Is (or was) the element real f*ck'n funny?

Here's what the yes/no answers to these three questions will tell you: 1. Is (or was) the element funny? Yes or No—Don't use the element because there are much stronger bits. 2. Is (or was) the element real funny? Yes or No—Don't use the element because there are stronger bits. 3. Is (or was) the element real f*ck'n funny? Yes—It's a killer bit: use it! If No—Don't use it; it must be killer. If a story, anecdote or piece of data isn't real f*ck'n funny or informative or compelling, then it's not strong enough to be used.

72

If you're traveling and have an extra hour or a free evening, call up some stations and offer to come in.

Pack an extra press kit or two when you are on the road. Often hosts are looking for something a little different and would welcome out of town, in-studio guests. Make a few cold calls. You might just wind up with a heated discussion on the air or you might offer to tape something for a station's use at a later date.

Don't blame the media in your presentation.

It's a bad idea to point fingers at the media either in your written material or on air. The only exception is if your organization makes its living by media critique. Although hosts often give the traditional media a lot of grief, they still consider themselves a part of the media. It is often a sweeping generalization and a cheap shot to blame your troubles on the media. If you have a very strong example of a specific incident, you might decide to use it. Otherwise, don't do it.

Make a list of the most important points that you want to make sure everyone knows.

Decide on the most important points that you want listeners to understand and remember. When President Clinton ran for office in 1992, his campaign staff ded in every speech and woven into every discussion of change. Find two to five points you want to somehow get across in every interview and make a check list. When practicing for your interview, find a way to work your points in without it seeming as if you were reviewing a check list. You will know you have reached your goal when you get all of your points across during an interview.

Do some practice interviews with your "host" asking you questions that have nothing to do with your subject matter. Find a subtle way to incorporate your points. Don't be obnoxious and say to your host "I'm really here to talk about x rather than y."

If your organization has an 800 number that you want callers to use, then be sure to mention the number at least twice while on the air. Rattling off the number once isn't of much use, but giving the number twice will yield calls. Similarly, if you have them, give out Web page and e-mail addresses.

Keep an ongoing "bag of options" available. This should include position papers, mission statement, articles you want to refer to. Keep them in a notebook and bring the notebook with you to all interviews. Let everyone know you work with that you are collecting material for your "bag of options." Have a box at your office that they can deliver material to or an e-mail address that they can send ideas to. Give a prize of luncheon to contributors.

Make sure you know and have READ your material.

As obvious as this seems, during the President's radio initiative for the Crime Bill—one of the Cabinet Secretaries admitted on the air to not having read the legislation. The host and listeners made chopped liver out of that Cabinet Secretary. Do your homework!

Only one in four Americans follows the news closely, so make sure you give the background about an issue.

A recent poll revealed that only one in four Americans follows news stories closely. Many people get news and views from talk radio so be sure to give a short but full background and history of your issue. Frame the story, making sure people get a complete picture and background of the issue and/or problem. Remember, just because you read the newspaper doesn't mean everyone else does.

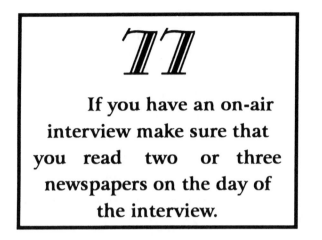

77

If you have an on-air interview make sure that you read two or three newspapers on the day of the interview.

Your host or news director will have read the papers, so it's important that you do. A good start is the local paper, *The New York Times, Washington Post, Washington Times* or *Los Angeles Times* and *USA Today.* If you can possibly relate your story to something in the newspapers, do it. It gives you common ground with your host and shows that you are well informed. If you're doing an interview by phone and don't have time to read the paper, have a staffer who has read the papers listen in on the interview with headphones. That person can then silently jot you notes about topics to address.

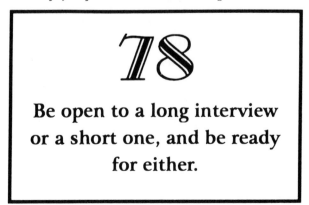

78

Be open to a long interview or a short one, and be ready for either.

A short interview where you make your points and make them well, can be much more memorable and often get more play (because they can be easily incorporated into later newscasts) than a longer interview that drags on and bores everyone. On the other hand, you should always have enough material for a longer interview as well. Be prepared to be on the air for a short three-minute interview, but have enough different and interesting material to make it an hour.

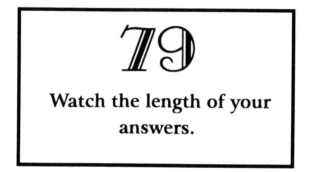

Watch the length of your answers.

Don't be long-winded or monosyllabic. Can the host get a question in between your answers? Do they have to break to shut you up? Or are your answers so short that the host has to work to get you to say anything? In general, anything more than thirty seconds is a very long answer. Pay attention to the flow of conversation between you and the host—you'll know when you're talking too much or too little. A good rule is to answer only what you've been asked. Of course, you want to weave your own pre-planned points into your responses, but should do so without going off on wild tangents and talking forever.

Be specific and answer questions with specifics if asked about them.

A high-level politician was asked to give some specifics on the companies he cited as examples of the policy under discussion. No matter how much the host prodded, he couldn't do it. An interview that could have been lively, with easily identifiable companies turned out to be more of the same political drivel. Use questions as springboards for your agenda and talking points—work them in, but not like the Presidential debates where they just avoided answering.

Welcome tough questions and be ready for them.

Answer all questions as non-defensively as possible. "I'm glad you brought that up" or "I'd be happy to answer that" or even "that's a tough question and I'm glad to have the opportunity to answer it" are all appropriate responses. It can be helpful to say, "You can quote me." Make sure that you can answer any kind of question about your organization in a non-defensive manner. Practice, practice, practice until you can answer as easily as you say, "good morning." Anxiety shows in voice intonation and pitch as well as body language.

A host will invariably bring up some fact, law or article that you didn't know about. If you don't know the facts or statistics, that's okay. Be honest about it and then get back to the host with information.

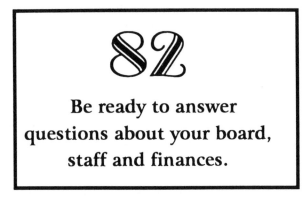

82

Be ready to answer questions about your board, staff and finances.

Think of your board and your masthead of management as your billboard. If there has ever been some question about a member of your organization, be ready to answer it. Anticipate that when you least expect it, someone is going to ask you about that person. Make sure that you know something about each person on your board, and that in their briefing materials there is a short bio with some notes about anything that might be asked. Try and use the negatives about a board member to your advantage. During a recent interview an ambassador was asked if being a political appointment was a disadvantage. The ambassador countered that because he had political experience, he was able to help the country's prime minister understand why the Clinton Administration had to make the political decisions they made.

Be ready to disclose where your money comes from and how you spend it. Hosts and callers alike want to know who are your big givers. If you're a politician a standard question is how much of your campaign money is from out of state or how much comes from "special interests" such as political action committees. For advocacy organizations, where your money comes from and how you spend it is a very big question. How much it costs you to raise the money and how big are the salaries are of the CEO and other staff are regular questions. If you are a single spokesperson, be honest about how you are able to do what you are doing. Be ready and not hesitant with your answers, even to the point of having a printed sheet available if asked. Make sure that you review this information with every member of your staff who deals with the public. Recently a spokesperson for breast implants was asked by some media members how her expenses were paid. She gave a different answer than the company's PR firm had given, and it ruined the credibility of the presentation.

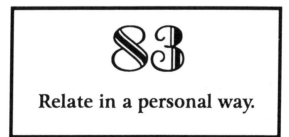

83

Relate in a personal way.

The sheer force of personality can carry you miles, but you still must always be ready to answer what is put to you. Tell stories and relate issues personally, but be sure you answer the question.

When talking to callers, use their first names. Barry Lynn, a radio host who is also the Executive Director of Americans for the Separation of Church and State, recommends calling callers by their first names because it shows respect for them and humanizes you. His example: "Marcy, you've got to listen to what I'm going to say, because you've got some wrong information."

You can interrupt the host if he or she is constantly talking. Be polite about interrupting. Depending on the host they might respect you more for it.

Use the name of your organization when you can. Use it often but not too often. You are there to sell your cause. If you don't use the name of your group no one will know who you are.

Whatever you do, don't lose your composure. Do WHATEVER you have to do to remain calm. Do not let the host or other guests rattle you. Come prepared for strategies to remain calm.

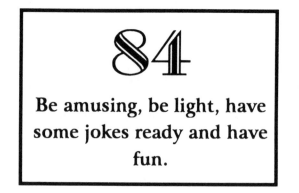

84

Be amusing, be light, have some jokes ready and have fun.

If you have no sense of humor, go to a local comedy club and ask a comedian to lighten up some of your speech material. Mark Katz of the Sound Bite Institute in New York is a master at this. Have one or two jokes that you can use on the air that make people laugh with you. Senator Bob Dole made light of his age by saying that he and Senator Strom Thurmond follow the same health plan so that, "If he eats a banana, I eat a banana." It deflected the Dole age issue and got people to laugh. Vice President Gore has one about tie breaking in the Senate, saying every time he votes he's on the winning side. It gives each of these men a human side, something that says "they're a little bit like me." Another technique is to quote from a cartoon, as long as you practice explaining the drawing so that the punch line makes sense and is funny.

The best hosts are excellent at pithy quotes and sound bites. Talk host Jim Bohannon tosses them off readily. Once while listening to a boring politician he leaned over and said "There's a minor tropical storm from that spin." If you can get an arsenal of these, use them. But, it is important to make the material fit you. Just because one person has a successful technique it doesn't mean that work for you. You are a different person.

Radio consultant Jim Tazareck says that people don't tune in the radio to have their day screwed up and make them depressed. Humor can carry you and your issue a long way. Think about the interview as an adventure, as a chance to get to know and to like the person you are talking to. Keep a light touch, even with difficult subjects. If you are discussing world hunger, it is inappropriate to be light on the air, but telling a story about how extraordinary humans can be in the face of obliterating adversity, can lighten up a tough story and get people beyond overwhelming emotions that they cause them to turn off and numb out.

A spokesperson who is willing to relax and have fun can make quite an impression, even if his or her issue doesn't get talked about. Senator Lieberman appeared on an FM personality show, with the goal of talking about more funding for the COPS program to combat crime. What happened instead of a talk about crime or even the specific program, endeared him to local listeners. He discussed the Yankees' farm team. He sang the Yankees song. He talked about how tough it is to represent Connecticut, a state split between fans of the Boston Red Sox and fans of the New York Yankees. In other words, he had fun and was a tremendous success.

If you are on a very conservative program you may (unless you are a politician) want to point out where there is agreement between the left and the right.

It can make things go a bit smoother if your host and listeners don't think that you're from Mars. There has been significant agreement between the left and the right about some issues of free speech, such as government regulation of the Internet, and agreement of excess in government in cases such as the Randy Weaver case at Ruby Ridge.

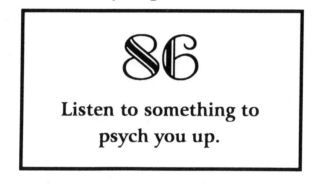

86

Listen to something to psych you up.

Be sure that you are not low energy on your interview. When you are not in the greatest mood for your interview, do something to psych yourself up—listen to your favorite music, call a friend who can get you pumped up, or read something that gets your juices flowing.

87

Leave egos at the door, they get magnified over the air.

Few people can pull off a grandiose ego—Rush Limbaugh can because he has a relationship with his audience. However, radio magnifies any tendency toward ego. A spokesperson known around Washington as an incredibly stuffed shirt did his thing on the air. Not only did he sound worse than you would imagine but as soon as the interview was finished and he hung up, the host roasted him. His whole presentation was wasted.

Don't be arrogant and think that being on the radio is easy. Have some respect for the skill of the hosts and don't make the mistake of under-preparing for an interview. A good host and savvy call-in listeners can provide quite a challenge if you haven't adequately prepared. Those old-timers from Alcoholics Anonymous have a great expression, "There are only two people who get me in trouble—the poor little me and the great I am." Words to live by for radio, too.

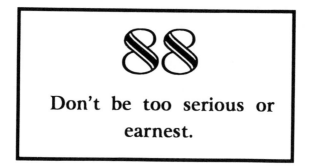

88

Don't be too serious or earnest.

Arrogance is a big problem but so is over earnestness. Recently, a well-known author was on a national show about a book he had written about children in the inner city. He was deadpan and serious. He clearly felt he was doing God's work and it came through. The urge to turn the radio off became overwhelming. Thinking that you can't get a smile even from a serious topic is really a problem. Think of being on the radio as one giant cocktail party. If everyone who comes up to you to talk to you hears about the anguish and pain of your work, you will soon be standing in a room alone. Yes, people do want to hear about your cause. A funny or heroic story that has a human element allows people to identify with you as a real person and goes a long way.

Political drivel is just that— find a way to say something that does not sound like a standard political stump speech.

Evaluate the listeners and the host. Most radio audiences are fairly sophisticated. When listeners hear the standard rhetoric, it makes them shut off their minds if not their radios. So when preparing your radio campaign, make sure that it has its own distinctive flavor. Take time to make sure that sweeping statements can be backed up, and that you can deliver your message with a fresh-sounding perspective.

90

Choose an in-studio
interview over a telephone
interview if you can
POSSIBLY do it.

It's great to just answer the phone to do a radio interview. You can do tons of stations that way. But if you're in the same city, even if it's just for a five-or 10-minute interview, do it in person because in-person chemistry is important. In addition:

You will develop a relationship with the host and producer—good for future interviews and issues.

- You have a better chance of getting longer air time.
- Your host (unless it's someone like Howard Stern) will be nicer to you, purely out of social convention.
- You have a better chance to assess the show and cement your future strategy.
- You may be able to bring supplementary materials, photos, etc., that will help make your case to the host who can help you convey it over the air. Be ready to have something to add at the end of the show. Something that summarizes your points and people will be able to remember.

- You have a better chance of getting a tape of the show, provided you bring a blank tape with you.

- You should inform friends or local organizations that you will be on the air, get them to call in. It will help counter negative callers.

- You should always behave as if the microphone is on—don't say anything to the producer or host that you would not want on the air.

- You will want to make sure you have some water next to you. You might need it. Stay far away from carbonated beverages.

- You may want to bring a camera. You could use a photo with the host or in the studio for future publicity. But always ask—it may be a "bad hair day" for the host.

91

If you are in the studio, pay attention to the host's body language. If you are on the phone pay attention to your voice intonation and the caller's.

This will give you clues on how to proceed and if you should continue with your line of discussion. Body language can tell you an enormous amount, and it's a good idea, if you can, to watch politicians in a room or on television. They are often the masters of this. You can learn some tricks of the trade.

Arthur Joseph, who created the Vocal Awareness Method, says that when we communicate with spoken language, only eight percent of that communication is received through words, the actual language of communication. About 37 percent is gathered from the sound of the voice and 55 percent is understood from body language. Therefore, if you are speaking on the telephone or over the air, 92 percent of your information is communicated solely through the sound of your voice, not the content. Voice exercises, and paying attention to your instrument, your voice, is crucial.

What makes someone or something believable? Answer: What would make you believe yourself?

When preparing for an on-air campaign, spend a fair amount of time figuring out how to make yourself believable. Listen to the radio and even watch interviews on TV. Listen to voice intonation, watch eye contact and body language. Ask yourself what's your gut reaction to the speaker? What makes the spokesperson believable or unbelievable? What are the issues in your campaign that are not going to fly? Are there any ways to make them more believable?

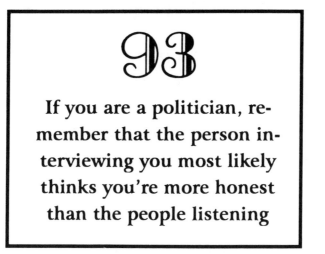

93

If you are a politician, remember that the person interviewing you most likely thinks you're more honest than the people listening

A *Times-Mirror* survey shows that the news media believes politicians are more honest than the general public does. This means your interviewer probably believes you to be more honest than the listeners do. Therefore, politicians must do something in the initial few minutes to establish their honesty with the audience. It's imperative that it is done in a non-defensive way. If you have a record of doing what you promised, weave that into the conversation, make it one of the main points you intend to get across in the interview.

94

If you are a public official, or head of an organization, make sure you acknowledge that you are influenced by phone calls, faxes, e-mail and letters you receive.

This does several things; it lets people know that they can write and call you and it lets them know that you know who pays your salary. Nobody likes a lone ranger politician. You can easily slip this into a discussion, "some of the mail and calls, I have been receiving lately . . ." or "I came into office with this in mind, but my constituents felt . . ." or "We had this policy at our agency. After hearing from the public, we took another look at that policy and . . . ."

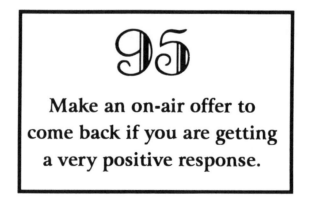

95

Make an on-air offer to come back if you are getting a very positive response.

If there are a lot of callers and they are not just calling to shoot you down and the host is very complimentary, you should offer to come back in the near future. This however, should not be a standard pat offer. Save it for when you know you're a winner.

8

Following-up After a Show

If the host or producer says,"we've got to have you back," don't assume you'll be back in two weeks.

Clarify what he or she means—two weeks, six weeks, six months or a year. Don't bug the producer, lots of times he or she was just being nice. Try and ascertain what is meant. Find out what subject they would like to have you back to discuss, and then follow up by sending some more information about that topic. Don't send so much information that they don't need you, but enough so that they maintain interest.

97

Thank you notes and calls are imperative.

Make sure you call the producer (and host if appropriate) after you have or your spokesperson has been on the air. You can leave a message, it is not always necessary to speak with the producer, they may not have the time. Then make sure you follow it up with a thank you note, as well as holiday cards.

98

Find a way to continue communicating with the producer or host and, if possible, with the listeners.

While on the air, jot down a few of the questions asked. Can you provide more information? Like a salesperson, use the interview as a chance to come back and provide more services. Send follow-up information via fax, messenger, e-mail or with a package. Just let them know what's going on with your issue without trying to book a guest.

9

Using the Internet

We now have what computer whiz Bob Vannass
refers to as the "death of distance." People from all over
the world can communicate via voice and word on the
Internet, and now there is an alternative way to get
your message out: accessing the Internet through various on-line services, and through various news groups.
You can engage in chat rooms or have live radio
(sound) or radio that is delayed via the Internet. It's a
great way to reach people who are involved and likely
to respond to an issue.

99

Establish relationships with the on-line providers.

On-line services can provide you lists of forums and forum leaders. Contact Genie, Compuserve, Delphi, Legi-Slate, Microsoft Network, America Online and Prodigy. Find the forums on your subject and see if you can arrange for your spokesperson to be a guest on them. In addition, your public relations department can participate in the forum discussions, raising your issues and promoting your spokesperson.

Keep in mind that most people who host on-line forums are not full time. Many do it as a volunteer job, and work in other places. Respect that their schedule may be different from yours and it may take longer to get a response from them. Again, anything you can do to make on-line hosts' jobs easier makes you a person with whom they want to work.

Get to know the people who lead the forums and who book the chats and the conferences on line. They can help you and even look out for your interests by letting you know when the on-line service is interested in a topic and when you might be able to get your spokesperson on. Just like relationships with producers, the relationship you establish with the on-line hosts can be your ticket to successful cyberspace publicity. At this point, the World Wide Web is ripe for political issues.

100

Set up a home page with sound attached.

You can "broadcast" regularly on the Internet. There are several packages available to allow you to convert tape to sound on the Internet. Try RealAudio. Many people have had great exposure with the Internet. It allows you to be your own radio station. And you can go one further by collecting e-mail addresses of interested people who are interested in receiving updates and information. Make sure you register your home page with Yahoo and other World Wide Web search engines.

101

Post e-mail on your subject.

Get on as many as possible e-mail lists on the World Wide Web. If you arrange to have a chat on line or choose to broadcast on-line, let other people know via the other chat rooms and through e-mail lists. Make sure that you are on e-mail lists so that you know what is going on. They are easy to get on, and don't waste a lot of paper. Be prepared to answer any e-mail that you get.

Last but not least—*Persistence is the Key*. Remember the races Abraham Lincoln lost **BEFORE** he became president!!!

10

Checklist For Effective Radio Promotion of Your Issue

Consider your current radio campaign or planned radio strategy. Then, answer the questions below by circling the YES or NO box. Feel free to photocopy these pages so that you can use this checklist again and again. To effectively mount a radio campaign of your issue or spokesperson, the answers to these questions should be Yes.

The question numbers are keyed to the numbered strategies and tips, so that if your answer is NO—or even if it's YES—you can gain guidance from the text.

Preparing the Message and the Campaign

YES NO 1. Is your spokeperson willing to go on the air?

YES NO 2. Have you listened to the media you want to use?

YES NO 3. Have you taken the time to define your issue and create your message?

YES NO 4. Are you using popular expressions and images?

YES NO 5. Are your goals measurable and obtainble?

YES NO 6. Is your campaign designed to move the middle voters?

YES NO 7. If you are preaching to the choir, is that your goal?

YES NO 8. Have you personalized your issue? Can people identify with your issue and spokesperson?

YES NO 9. Have you made complex situations/issue understandable?

YES NO 10. Have you piggybacked your issue on hot news and current events?

YES NO 11. Have you allowed enough time to make your campaign work?

YES NO 12. Have you offered alternatives that reduce people's fears?

YES NO 13. Have you assessed whether the timing is right for your campaign to be successful?

YES NO 14. Have you found a way to make your story news today?

YES NO 15. Do you have a catch phrase—something people will remember?

YES NO 16. Are you being creative in your use of statistics?

YES NO 17. Have you thought out the pros and cons of your strategy and message?

YES NO 18. Are you taking into account the general mood of the American public?

YES NO 19. Have you addressed common stereotypes about Democrats and liberals?

YES NO 20. Is your spokesperson likeable?

YES NO 21. Does your spokesperson have a good radio voice?

YES NO 22. Does your spokesperson know and understand the background material you are sending out?

YES NO 23. Does your spokesperson listen to talk radio?

YES NO 24. Do you do things in such a way as to give your operation a touch of class?

Marketing a Campaign, Issue Or
Spokesperson

YES NO 25. Have you developed any clever games or giveaways? Are you doing anything wild that will attract attention?

YES NO 26. Do you have a good press kit?

YES NO 27. Have you considered setting up an actuality line?

YES NO 28. If your organization's history includes something worth highlighting in a marketing effort, have you used it?

YES NO 29. Have you planned a part of your campaign that is regularly scheduled and fun?

YES NO 30. Can you create an event that hosts and producers will want to cover? Have you made it easy for them to cover it?

YES NO 31. Have you sent relevant information out in addition to your press kit? Do you send it regularly?

YES NO 32. Have you considered putting your talking points on a card to send out?

YES NO 33. Can you provide a planning calendar to hosts and stations?

YES NO 34. Have you done research into the stations and areas you will be working with?

YES NO 35. Do you have a book or booklet that can be used along with your campaign?

YES NO 36. Are there some volunteers you can get to listen to talk radio and call into shows on your issues?

YES NO 37. Have you thought of getting an 800 number?

YES NO 38. Have you thought about coordinating your campaign with like-minded organizations?

YES NO 39. Are you willing to debate the other side?

YES NO 40. If you can't get the other side on the air, have you considered issuing a challenge?

Booking A Spokesperson

YES NO 41. Are you willing to book on all kinds of shows and formats?

YES NO 42. Have you considered scheduling a morning drive tour for a hot spokesperson or issue?

YES NO 43. Is the person pitching your campaign to producers both knowledgeable and personable?

YES NO 44. Do you follow up your pitch call with other materials?

YES NO 45. Does your pitch letter answer the big question of WHY this issue NOW?

YES NO 46. Are you supporting your faxes with follow-up phone calls?

YES NO 47. Have you considered an on-air conference call with several hosts and news stations?

YES NO 48. Does your pitch highlight the areas of current controversy?

YES NO 49. Do you understand the hours talk radio people work and are you, or your staff, willing to work those hours also?

YES NO 50. Can you provide a choice in spokespeople?

YES NO 51. If you have to cancel, can you provide a good substitute? Do you apologize in writing if you have to cancel?

Cultivating Relationships With Producers And Hosts

YES NO 52. Do you invite the press to your events and social gatherings to in order spend time with them in informal settings? Have you taken steps to become part of the radio community?

YES NO 53. Are you aware of, and sensitive to, hosts' needs?

YES NO 54. Are you honest with producers and hosts?

YES NO 55. Have you developed relationships with radio people in small markets?

YES NO 56. Are you careful not to annoy producers for too much stuff?

YES NO 57. Do you understand the importance of the First Amendment and of not asking hosts about their political beliefs?

YES NO 58. Do you try to help hosts and producers in their careers?

YES NO 59. Are you unfailingly polite in your dealings with hosts and producers?

YES NO 60. Do you know when to give up trying to book a particular guest or show?

YES NO 61. When you are leaking information or giving a "heads up" do you include radio stations?

YES NO 62. Are you willing to help stations with their information needs off the air as well as on?

YES NO 63. Do you send written confirmations of your bookings?

YES NO 64. Do you try to use a personal touch with each host and producer?

Being an Effective Spokesperson

YES NO 65. Is some of your information different from the current political spin?

YES NO 66. Are you able to articulate what would happen if your stand on an issue becomes policy? Can you articulate what would happen if your opponent's strategy were implemented?

YES NO 67. Do you know what the other side is saying?

YES NO 68. Is your organization credible? Are you able to deal appropriately with any skeletons in your closet?

YES NO 69. Are you able to succinct with your message?

YES NO 70. Can you counter the opposition point-by-point?

YES NO 71. Do you have a way to evaluate the impact of any item (story, anecdote or fact) used on the air?

YES NO 72. Have you considered calling some stations when you're traveling and have some free time to do a show?

YES NO 73. Are you careful not to blame the media in your presentation?

YES NO 74. Have you made a list of the most important points you want to convey?

YES NO 75. Have you read the relevant material?

YES NO 76. Can you give the background about an issue, for the listeners who don't know the issue?

YES NO 77. If you have an on-air interview, have you read two or three newspapers on the day of the interview?

YES NO 78. Are you prepared for either a short or long interview?

YES NO 79. Are you aware of the length of your answers and the flow of the conversation between you and your host?

YES NO 80. Can you answer specific questions with specific information?

YES NO 81. Are you ready for tough questions? Do you welcome them?

YES NO 82. Can you answer questions about your board and staff? Are you ready to disclose where your money comes from and how it is spent?

YES NO 83. Do you try to relate to listeners in a personal way?

YES NO 84. Do you have an arsenal of jokes ready? Are you willing to have fun?

YES NO 85. Are you willing to point out the places of agreement between the left and the right, if you're on a very conservative program?

YES NO 86. Have you psyched yourself up?

YES NO 87. Have you left your ego at the door? Do you have respect for the art of radio?

YES NO 88. Are you careful not to be overearnest in your presentation?

YES NO 89. Is your presentation fresh and interesting?

YES NO 90. When possible, have you chosen an in-studio interview?

YES NO 91. Do you pay attention to the host's body language or voice intonation?

YES NO 92. Is your campaign believable? Do you believe it?

YES NO 93. Have you prepared for the fact that most Americans don't believe politicians?

YES NO 94. If you are a politician, do you acknowledge how you are affected by phone calls and mail?

YES NO 95. Are you willing to make an on-air offer to come back?

YES NO 96. Do you understand that a host or producer's invitation to return might not mean an immediate booking?

Following-up After a Show

YES NO 97. Do you send thank you notes and make thank you calls to producers and hosts?

YES NO 98. After a show, have you figured out ways to continue communicating with producers and hosts?

Using the Internet

YES NO 99. Have you established relationships with on-line providers?

YES NO 100. Have you considered putting up a home page with sound attached?

YES NO 101. Do you or does your organization regularly post e-mail on your issue?

11

Tips For Television

Most of the points in this book can be used for booking television and for planning stategy. However, there are some specific points when you are going to be a guest on television.

How to Dress

- Generally, choose business clothing—do not over dress, think of your audience—is it housewives or business types?

- Try taking a photo of yourself sitting in the clothes you want to wear before making a decision on what to wear. Show it to people you trust and get their opinion.

- Do not wear lots of jewelry- lots of gold or silver and large jewelry shines and distracts-when in doubt, take it off.

- Wear colors-stay away from black and white. There is a debate about men wearing white shirts. They did in the Presidential debates, but you may want to go with a light color.

- Do not choose clothes that are the height of fashion- be a little more conservative Obviously, MTV and *Face the Nation* play to different audiences.

- Avoid plaids and checks.

- Button down collars do not look as neat on TV.

- Men—make sure you are wearing long socks.

- Wear bright and slightly bold ties.

- Men should sit on their jacket tails.

- Let the station put powder on you—there is nothing worse than shine and grease. Buy a small compact (men too) and put it on eyes, cheekbones, forehead and nose. You may also want to rub your face with a damp paper towel before the powder.

- Not too heavy with eye makeup, but more makeup than usual.
- If you are going out of town for a television interview, take a change of cloths. Many a cup of coffee has been spilled on the plane. Many pairs of stockings have been run right before air time.

What to ask:

- Ask what angle you are going to be shot from
- Ask if a show will be taped or live, if taped, treat it as if it were live
- Ask where to look in the camera
- Be sure to look at the host, unless there is a different camera for call-ins
- Find out how long you will be on the air and for how many segments
- Ask who the host is and who the other guests are. If you have time, research the other guests
- Always ask to see how you will be fonted. Look at it.
- Ask to hear how you will be introduced.
- Be sure to tell the producers if you are very short or tall ahead of time so they can adjust the chairs.
- Find out if you are going to be part of a satellite interview, and if you will be able to see the other guests or just hear them.

On the Set

- When the host introduces you—nod. You may want to say hi, perhaps ask a light hearted question of the host or even make a statement. It will help you get control of the interview.
- Do not smile too much, act yourself.
- Make sure you are talking in sound bites, but not too short Q: How is the economy? A: Well versus "It is doing well because . . ."
- If someone is opposite you, don't wait for your host to ask your opinion, jump in.
- If your issue is going to impact people at home, look at the camera and say: "You are going to be effected by this, call or write your member of congress."
- Make believe you are talking to friends and/or colleagues.
- If the set is small, do not lean into it too much, it will block the camera shots.
- Practice before each show and on each topic.
- Watch your microphone—make sure you and/or your jewelry does not bump against it.
- Do not drink a lot during the show.

o Remember that radio is a hotter medium than TV. Don't overwhelm with motion or voice.

- Watch the hosts hand signals to you- this will let you know when the host needs to take a break etc.

- Watch your hand gestures, use your hands to make a point. Do not overuse them.

- Ignore the floor director- do not let him or her distract you.

- Be aware of breaks and commercials—do not be upset if the host cuts you off

- When doing a satellite feed—see yourself as talking to a live audience—it will help you be less rigid. You may hear without seeing. Stay focused, and maintain your energy level. Even if your not talking, look engaged and not bored.

Other Tips

- Choose in-studio interviews rather than satellite interviews if you have a choice.

- Send information about you and your topic before you get to the studio—scripts are often written in advance.

- Don't send anyone for an interview that is not pleasing to look at

- If you see a story call the Senior Producer or the News Director, find out who the contact person is, and pitch your view.

- Do not eat in the green room- food can get stuck in your teeth.

- Even if you are not invited as a guest you can fax in clear talking points. Remember that these are NOT the same as a press release.

12

Tips For Print Interviews

- Be honest and tell the truth o A photo may be taken- dress appropriately.
- Do not say things off the record or on background.
- Tape the conversation, but don't appear to do it out of mistrust or have someone else present at the interview. Try not to meet alone. For a phone interview, you may want to have a staff member listen in on the conversation.
- Speak slowly—the interviewer is taking notes.
- Emphasize and/or repeat important points.
- Organize your thoughts BEFORE the interview

- Do not think too much about your answers. Give the reporter the answer they want. If they failed to ask the right question, answer that too.

- Follow up if you do not have an immediate answer and be sure you do follow up.

- If something embarrassing comes up, get it out of the way first. Tell your staff/boardafter the interview.

- Forward any back-up material and send a note if you have a quote or statistics or other information. The note or fax can say: "Thank you for the interview. I checked the numbers I quoted you and they are in fact." Or you could clarify that "I checked the spelling on and it is . . ."

- Treat it as an on camera or radio interview (anything you say goes on the air).

- Don't be friends with the reporter, although you can be friendly. Don't let the reporter become friends with you.

- As with radio and television interviews, send a thank-you note.

- Feel free to send in material to a reporter who covers your issues or write an article about your issue.

13

Who is Listening to Talk Radio?

When comparing talk radio audiences to other radio formats, talk radio audiences are much more likely to...
- have an income over $75,000 (21% -vs-14%)
- have graduated college (50% -vs- 35%)
- read a newspaper daily (91% -vs- 74%)
- own their residence (78% -vs- 69%)

1994, Simmons Market Research Bureau

Talk Radio listeners are much more likely to use the Internet.
(45% -vs- 32% for the general population)

1996, Pew Research Center

On a variety of liberal and conservative issues - talk radio listeners opinions mirrored those of the general population.

1993, Times Mirror Expressions of Public Opinions

Radio was the second most used source of candidate information in the 1996 New Hampshire Primary.

1996, The Edison Poll

While 30% of the talk radio audience labels itself "Conservative" or "Ultra Conservative", only 18% of the audience labels itself "Liberal" or "Ultra Liberal".

1995, Talkers Magazine

65% of 1996 New Hampshire Primary voters said they listen to talk radio.

1996, The Edison Poll

Call-In Political Talk Radio: Background, Content, Audiences, Portrayal In Mainstream Media - Executive Summary
Annenberg Public Policy Center of the University of Pennsylvania

18% of the adult population reports listening to at least one call-in political talk radio show at least twice a week.

Regular political talk radio listeners are more likely than non-listeners to consume all types of news media (excepting TV news), to be more knowledgeable about politics and social issues, and to be involved in political activities.

Talk radio is not monolithic. Rather, its content is varied. In general, conservative shows are more likely to focus on foreign and military affairs than do the other shows; moderate/liberal shows focus more on family and education than the other types of political talk radio.

Political talk radio listeners are more critical of the mainstream media than are non-listeners.

Content analysis of seven weeks of Limbaugh (105 Hours), 150 hours of other hosts, and analysis of a stratified sample of more than 2500 newspaper articles about political talk radio suggest that:

- By focusing on extreme moments of talk radio without indicating how typical they are of the most widely heard shows, mainstream news may invite the inference that political talk radio is, at its best, routinely uncivil, and at worst, downright dangerous.

- By focusing on moments in which talk radio may have mobilized citizens or influenced legislation but not on those in which it failed to do so, newspaper articles on talk radio may exaggerate its impact.

- News articles overstate the homogeneity of political talk radio.

Voters News Service
November 5, 1996

Exit Polling: 36% of those Voting on Election Day
are Frequent Listeners to Talk Radio

n = 4,146

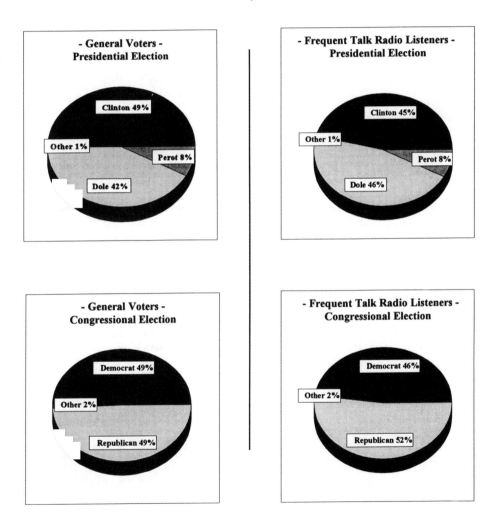

1996 Pre-Election Voting Survey (cont.)
Frequent Talk Radio Listeners -vs- Non-Listeners
Copyright April 1996, The Pew Research Center,
"Democratic Congressional Prospects Improve"

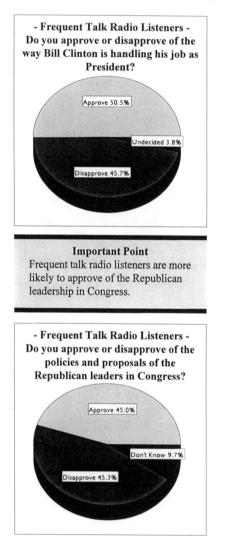

- Frequent Talk Radio Listeners -
Do you approve or disapprove of the
way Bill Clinton is handling his job as
President?

Approve 50.5%

Undecided 3.8%

Disapprove 45.7%

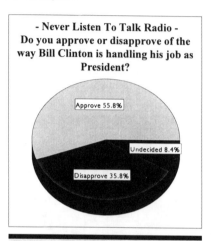

- Never Listen To Talk Radio -
Do you approve or disapprove of the
way Bill Clinton is handling his job as
President?

Approve 55.8%

Undecided 8.4%

Disapprove 35.8%

Important Point
Frequent talk radio listeners are more
likely to approve of the Republican
leadership in Congress.

Important Point
People who never listen to talk radio
are more likely to approve of Clinton's
leadership as President.

- Frequent Talk Radio Listeners -
Do you approve or disapprove of the
policies and proposals of the
Republican leaders in Congress?

Approve 45.0%

Don't Know 9.7%

Disapprove 45.3%

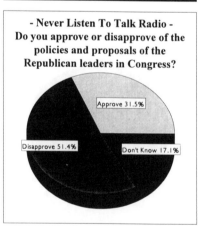

- Never Listen To Talk Radio -
Do you approve or disapprove of the
policies and proposals of the
Republican leaders in Congress?

Approve 31.5%

Disapprove 51.4%

Don't Know 17.1%

1996 Pre-Election Voting Survey
Frequent Talk Radio Listeners -vs- Non-Listeners
Copyright April 1996, The Pew Research Center,
"Democratic Congressional Prospects Improve"

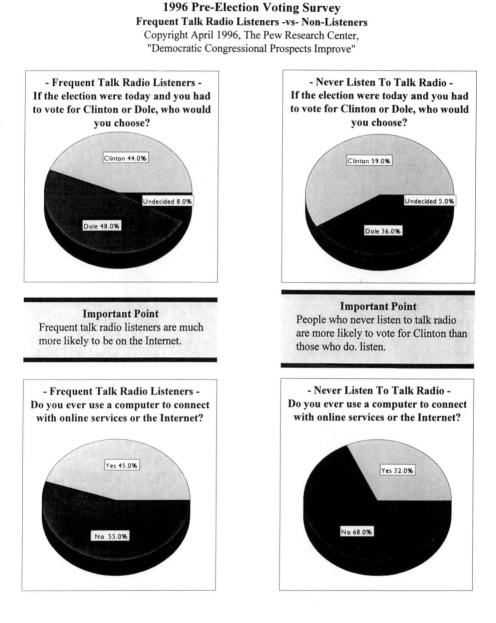

- Frequent Talk Radio Listeners -
If the election were today and you had
to vote for Clinton or Dole, who would
you choose?

Clinton 44.0%

Undecided 8.0%

Dole 48.0%

- Never Listen To Talk Radio -
If the election were today and you had
to vote for Clinton or Dole, who would
you choose?

Clinton 59.0%

Undecided 5.0%

Dole 36.0%

Important Point
Frequent talk radio listeners are much
more likely to be on the Internet.

Important Point
People who never listen to talk radio
are more likely to vote for Clinton than
those who do. listen.

- Frequent Talk Radio Listeners -
Do you ever use a computer to connect
with online services or the Internet?

Yes 45.0%

No 55.0%

- Never Listen To Talk Radio -
Do you ever use a computer to connect
with online services or the Internet?

Yes 32.0%

No 68.0%

The Media and Campaign 96
The Freedom Forum/Media Studies Center
Briefing, Number 1, April 1996
n=2,007

Source: Media Studies Center/Ruper Survey on Voters & Media Sept. 1996

How Voters Obtain Election Information

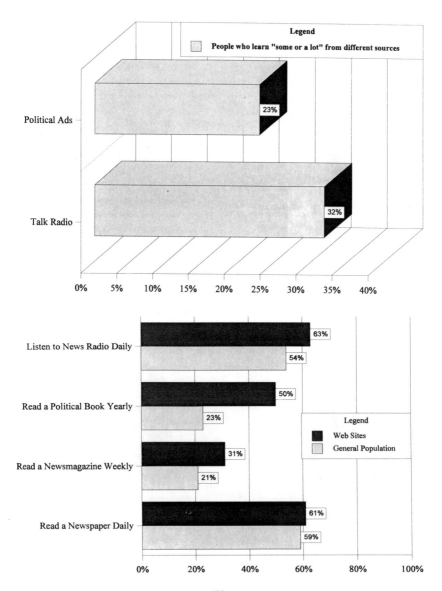

The Media and Campaign 96
The Freedom Forum/Media Studies Center
Briefing, Number 1, April 1996
n=2,0007

**Young voters get their information from
different sources than older voters**

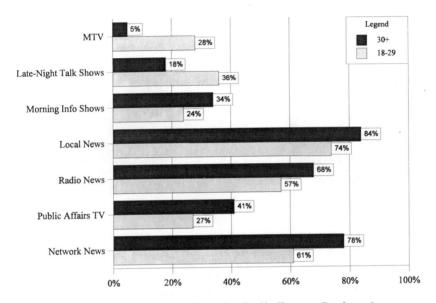

Listener Demographic Data By Radio Format Preferred
Total Population -vs- Talk Radio Listeners
Copyright Simmons Market Research Bureau 1994 Study of Media and Markets

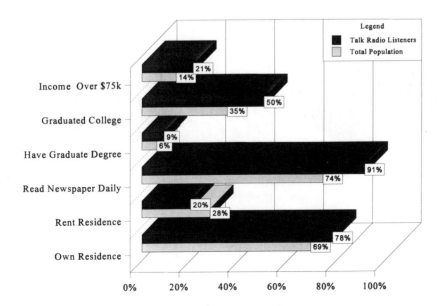

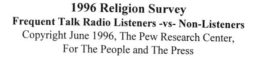

1996 Religion Survey
Frequent Talk Radio Listeners -vs- Non-Listeners
Copyright June 1996, The Pew Research Center,
For The People and The Press

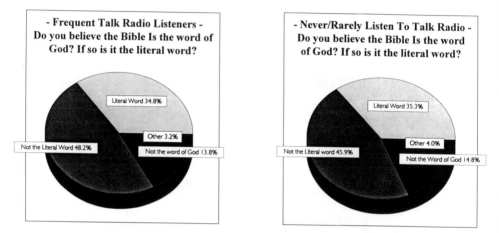

- Frequent Talk Radio Listeners -
Do you believe the Bible Is the word of
God? If so is it the literal word?

Literal Word 34.8%
Other 3.2%
Not the Literal Word 48.2%
Not the word of God 13.8%

- Never/Rarely Listen To Talk Radio -
Do you believe the Bible Is the word
of God? If so is it the literal word?

Literal Word 35.3%
Other 4.0%
Not the Literal word 45.9%
Not the Word of God 14.8%

Important Point
Whether you use liberal or conservative bellwethers, surveys constantly report that talk
radio listeners are remarkably representative of the total population.

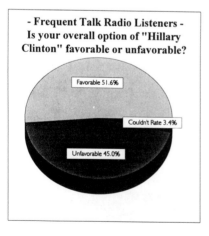

- Frequent Talk Radio Listeners -
Is your overall option of "Hillary
Clinton" favorable or unfavorable?

Favorable 51.6%
Couldn't Rate 3.4%
Unfavorable 45.0%

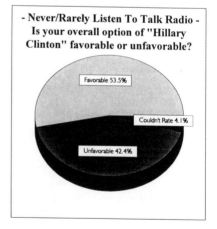

- Never/Rarely Listen To Talk Radio -
Is your overall option of "Hillary
Clinton" favorable or unfavorable?

Favorable 53.5%
Couldn't Rate 4.1%
Unfavorable 42.4%

1996 Religion Survey (cont.)
Frequent Talk Radio Listeners -vs- Non-Listeners
Copyright June 1996, The Pew Research Center,
For The People and The Press

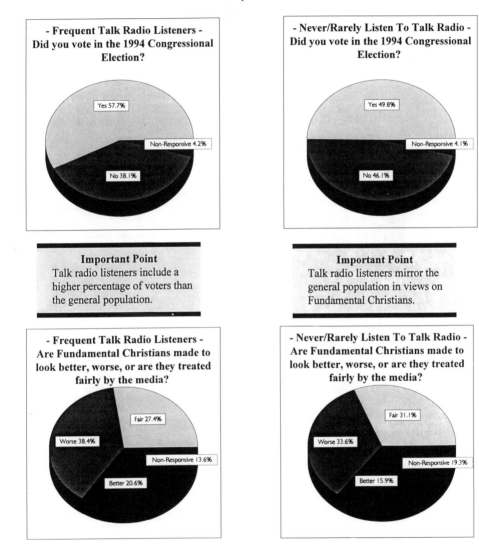

- Frequent Talk Radio Listeners -
Did you vote in the 1994 Congressional Election?

Yes 57.7%
Non-Responsive 4.2%
No 38.1%

- Never/Rarely Listen To Talk Radio -
Did you vote in the 1994 Congressional Election?

Yes 49.8%
Non-Responsive 4.1%
No 46.1%

Important Point
Talk radio listeners include a higher percentage of voters than the general population.

Important Point
Talk radio listeners mirror the general population in views on Fundamental Christians.

- Frequent Talk Radio Listeners -
Are Fundamental Christians made to look better, worse, or are they treated fairly by the media?

Fair 27.4%
Worse 38.4%
Non-Responsive 13.6%
Better 20.6%

- Never/Rarely Listen To Talk Radio -
Are Fundamental Christians made to look better, worse, or are they treated fairly by the media?

Fair 31.1%
Worse 33.6%
Non-Responsive 19.3%
Better 15.9%

1996 New Hampshire Primary Exit Polling
Copyright 1996, The Edison Poll, Inc.

The Edison Poll

- Interviewed 2501 voters as they left 25 randomly selected polling locations throughout New Hampshire.
- 1778 Republican primary voters and 723 Democratic primary voters were interviewed.
- Results were weighted to adjust for non-response by age and sex.

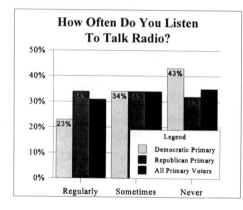

Important Point
While Republican Primary voters echoed the general population with time spent listening to talk radio - Democratic Primary voters listened less.

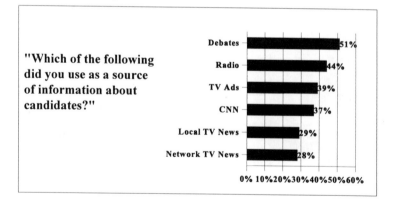

"Which of the following did you use as a source of information about candidates?"

- Debates — 51%
- Radio — 44%
- TV Ads — 39%
- CNN — 37%
- Local TV News — 29%
- Network TV News — 28%

0% 10% 20% 30% 40% 50% 60%

1996 New Hampshire Primary Exit Polling (cont.)
Copyright 1996, The Edison Poll, Inc.

How Talk Shows Influenced The Vote
Republican -vs- Democratic Primaries

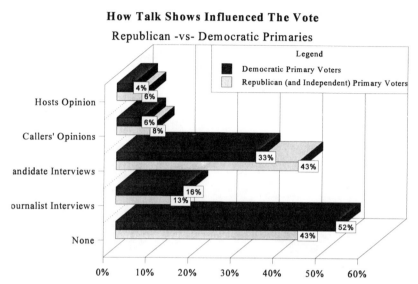

Presidential Priorities
Republican -vs- Democratic Primaries

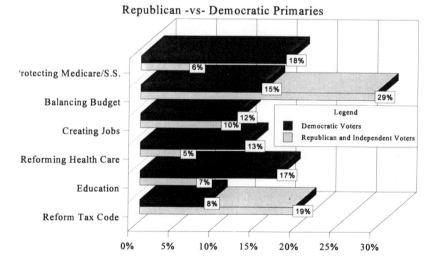

Talk Radio Listener Knowledge Of The Government
Excerpted from "Why Don't Americans Trust the Government"
Copyright 1996, The Washington Post/Kaiser Family Foundation/
Harvard University Survey Project

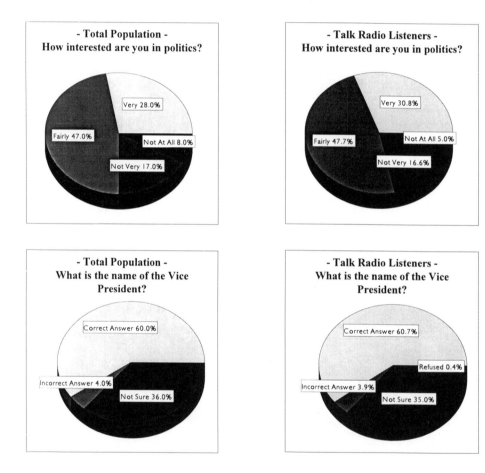

- Total Population -
How interested are you in politics?

Very 28.0%
Fairly 47.0%
Not At All 8.0%
Not Very 17.0%

- Talk Radio Listeners -
How interested are you in politics?

Very 30.8%
Fairly 47.7%
Not At All 5.0%
Not Very 16.6%

- Total Population -
What is the name of the Vice President?

Correct Answer 60.0%
Incorrect Answer 4.0%
Not Sure 36.0%

- Talk Radio Listeners -
What is the name of the Vice President?

Correct Answer 60.7%
Refused 0.4%
Incorrect Answer 3.9%
Not Sure 35.0%

Talk Radio Listener Knowledge Of The Government (cont.)
Excerpted from "Why Don't Americans Trust the Government"
Copyright 1996, The Washington Post/Kaiser Family Foundation/
Harvard University Survey Project

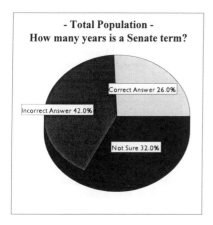

- Total Population -
How many years is a Senate term?

Correct Answer 26.0%
Incorrect Answer 42.0%
Not Sure 32.0%

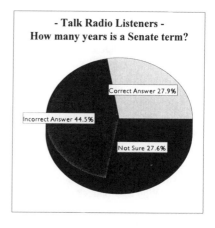

- Talk Radio Listeners -
How many years is a Senate term?

Correct Answer 27.9%
Incorrect Answer 44.5%
Not Sure 27.6%

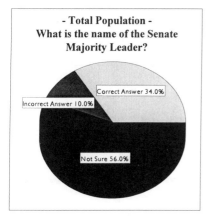

- Total Population -
What is the name of the Senate
Majority Leader?

Correct Answer 34.0%
Incorrect Answer 10.0%
Not Sure 56.0%

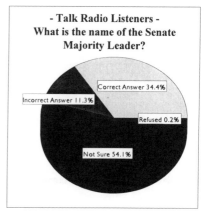

- Talk Radio Listeners -
What is the name of the Senate
Majority Leader?

Correct Answer 34.4%
Incorrect Answer 11.3%
Refused 0.2%
Not Sure 54.1%

1995 Political Issues Survey
Frequent Talk Radio Listeners -vs- Non-Listeners
Copyright November 1995, Times Mirror Center for People and the Press
"Voter Anxiety Dividing GOP; Energized Dems Backing Clinton"
N=2,000

- Frequent Talk Radio Listeners -
Top Three Sources of Dissatisfaction

#1 Economy (24%)
#2 Political System (21% tie)
#2 Health Care System (21%

- Never Listen To Talk Radio -
Top Three Sources of Dissatisfaction

#1 Health Care System (22%)
#2 Economy (19%)
#3 Political System (14%)

- Frequent Talk Radio Listeners -
Who Is to Blame?

#1 Congress (41%)
#2 People Themselves (23%)
#3 President (8%)

- Never Listen To Talk Radio -
Who Is to Blame?

#1 People Themselves (32%)
#2 Congress (31%)
#3 Business (8%)

- Frequent Talk Radio Listeners -
Party ID

Change	Party	Mar '95	Oct '95
-	Rep	47%	33%
+	Dem	22%	28%
+	Ind	30%	36%

- Never Listen To Talk Radio-
Party ID

Change	Party	Mar '95	Oct '95
-	Rep	32%	29%
-	Dem	30%	29%
+	Ind	33%	37%

The 1995 Talk Radio Audience
Copyright 1995, Talkers Magazine, Inc.

Sex	
Male	58%
Female	42%

Age	
12-17	2%
18-34	13%
35-44	18%
45-54	25%
55-64	27%
65+	15%

Ethnicity	
White	67%
Black	20%
Hispanic	8%
Asian	3%
Other	2%

Voted 1994	
Yes	70%
No	30%

Political Party	
Republican	31%
Democrat	19%
Libertarian	7%

Education	
Didn't Finish H.S.	7%
High School Graduate	20%
1 Year College	15%
2 Years College	17%
3 Years College	10%
College Graduate	16%
Attended Graduate School	15%

Annual Household Income	
Under $20k	8%
$20k-$30k	10%
$30k-$40k	10%
$40k-$50k	15%
$50k-$60k	15%
$60k-$70k	15%
$70k-$80k	10%
$80k-$90k	10%
$90k-$100k	5%
$100k+	2%

Political Philosophy	
"Ultra Conservative"	10%
"Conservative"	20%
"Fiscal Conservative/ Social Liberal"	17%
"Liberal"	15%
"Ultra Liberal"	3%
"Depends on Issue"	10%

1994 Format Preferences Survey
Paragon Research, May 1994

400 adults were surveyed
57% considered themselves "frequent" talk show listeners
43% considered themselves "occasional" listeners

How Much Do You Like Each Format? 1=Very Little				10=Very Much
	Total	Males	Females	Frequent Listeners	Occasional Listeners
Local talk shows	6.7	6.7	6.7	7.4	5.8
Controversial talk shows	6.1	6.1	6	6.4	5.6
Political talk shows	5.3	5.5	5	5.7	4.7
Consumer advocate talk shows	5.3	5.1	5.7	5.5	5.1
National talk shows	5.2	5.2	5.2	5.3	5
Sports talk shows	4.3	5.2	2.9	4.5	4
Counseling talk shows	3.9	3.1	5.1	3.8	4

1994 Election Nationwide Exit Poll
Total Population -vs- Frequent Talk Radio Listeners
Copyright 1994 Voter News Service

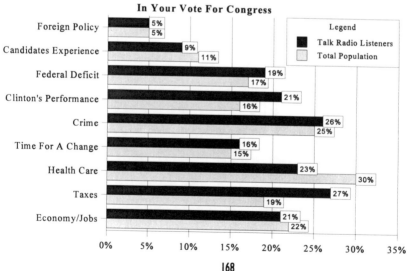

Which 1 Or 2 Of These Mattered Most In Your Vote For Congress

Listener Demographic Data By Radio Format Preferred
Total Population -vs- Talk Radio Listeners
Copyright Simmons Market Research Bureau 1994 Study of Media and Markets

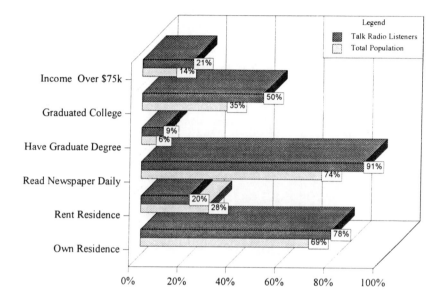

1994 Election Nationwide Exit Poll
Total Population -vs- Frequent Talk Radio Listeners
Copyright 1994 Voter News Service

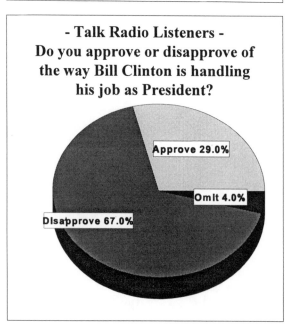

- Total Population -
Do you approve or disapprove of
the way Bill Clinton is handling
his job as President?

Approve 44.0%

Omit 4.0%

Disapprove 52.0%

- Talk Radio Listeners -
Do you approve or disapprove of
the way Bill Clinton is handling
his job as President?

Approve 29.0%

Omit 4.0%

Disapprove 67.0%

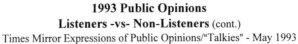

1993 Public Opinions
Listeners -vs- Non-Listeners (cont.)
Times Mirror Expressions of Public Opinions/"Talkies" - May 1993

How do you feel about restricting the sale of handguns?

How do you feel about proposals to allow gays and lesbians to serve in the military?

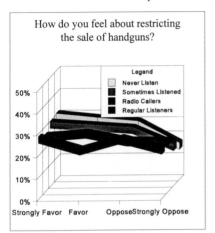

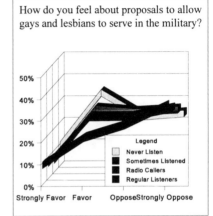

How do you feel about restricting the sale of handguns?					
	Strongly Favor	**Favor**	**Oppose**	**Strongly Oppose**	**N**
Total	28%	27%	25.6%	16.8%	4738
Regular Listeners	27.3%	21.7%	26.8%	21.8%	817
Radio Callers	25.1%	26.4%	22.7%	22.4%	602
Sometimes Listeners	28.3%	26.9%	25.5%	17.5%	1180
Never Listen	29.2%	27.2%	25.4%	15.2%	1817
How do you feel about proposals to allow gays and lesbians in the military?					
Total	7.8%	29.5%	25.6%	26.7%	4738
Regular Listeners	8.9%	21.1%	26.9%	35.9%	817
Radio Callers	6.9%	27.7%	27.9%	31.8%	602
Sometimes Listeners	5.4%	28.9%	27.3%	28.4%	1180
Never Listen	9.4%	33.5%	22.2%	23.7%	1817

1993 Public Opinions
Listeners -vs- Non-Listeners (cont.)
Times Mirror Expressions of Public Opinions/"Talkies" - May 1993

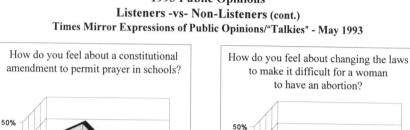

How do you feel about a constitutional amendment to permit prayer in schools?

How do you feel about changing the laws to make it difficult for a woman to have an abortion?

How do you feel about a constitutional amendment to permit prayer in schools?				
	Strongly Favor	Favor	Oppose	Strongly Oppose	N
Total	31.0%	37.9%	19.2%	7.4%	4738
Regular Listeners	33.8%	38.2%	17.0%	6.8%	817
Radio Callers	36.9%	35.6%	16.7%	6.2%	602
Sometimes Listeners	33.3%	32.0%	20.9%	8.8%	1180
Never Listen	30.1%	38.6%	18.9%	8.0%	1817
How do you feel about changing the laws to make it difficult for a woman to have an abortion?				
Total	14.7%	16.8%	35.2%	25.4%	4738
Regular Listeners	13.8%	15.6%	33.0%	29.2%	817
Radio Callers	15.9%	14.5%	30.8%	31.4%	602
Sometimes Listeners	17.1%	15.9%	36.2%	25.4%	1180
Never Listen	14.4%	17.1%	35.0%	26.0%	1817

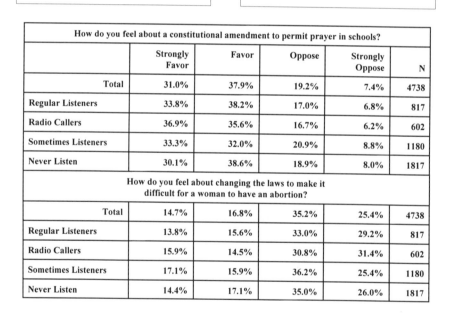

1993 Profile of Talk Radio Audience
Time/CNN Poll February, 1993

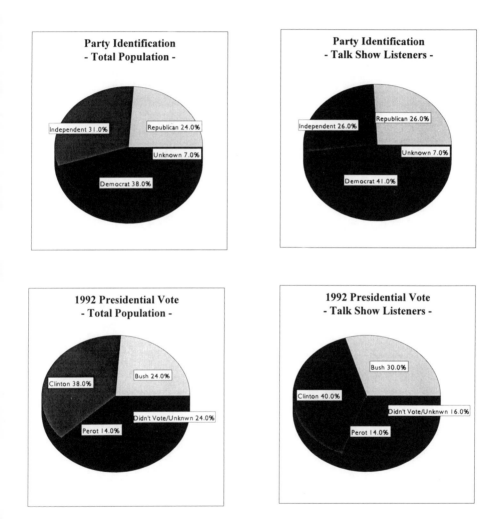

**Party Identification
- Total Population -**

Independent 31.0% Republican 24.0%
Unknown 7.0%
Democrat 38.0%

**Party Identification
- Talk Show Listeners -**

Independent 26.0% Republican 26.0%
Unknown 7.0%
Democrat 41.0%

**1992 Presidential Vote
- Total Population -**

Clinton 38.0% Bush 24.0%
Didn't Vote/Unknwn 24.0%
Perot 14.0%

**1992 Presidential Vote
- Talk Show Listeners -**

Clinton 40.0% Bush 30.0%
Didn't Vote/Unknwn 16.0%
Perot 14.0%

173

1993 Profile of Talk Radio Audience
Time/CNN Poll February, 1993

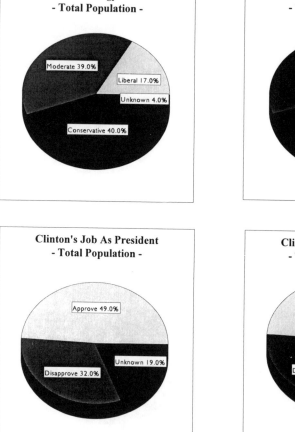

Ideology
- Total Population -

Moderate 39.0%
Liberal 17.0%
Unknown 4.0%
Conservative 40.0%

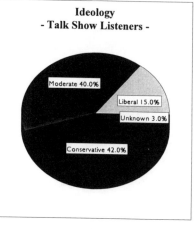

Ideology
- Talk Show Listeners -

Moderate 40.0%
Liberal 15.0%
Unknown 3.0%
Conservative 42.0%

Clinton's Job As President
- Total Population -

Approve 49.0%
Unknown 19.0%
Disapprove 32.0%

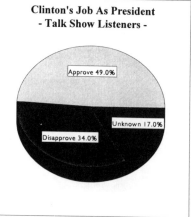

Clinton's Job As President
- Talk Show Listeners -

Approve 49.0%
Unknown 17.0%
Disapprove 34.0%

1993 Talk Radio Survey
The Vocal Minority in American Politics
Times Mirror Center for the People and the Press, July 1993

How Many Are Listening?
- 61% say they have listened
- 42% say they listen "regularly" or "sometimes"
- 23% say they listened "yesterday" or "today"
- 17% say they listen "regularly"

Total respondents: 1507

How Many Are Calling and Talking?
- 11% say they have tried to call in
- 6% say they have talked on the air
- 3% say they have talked on the air in the last year
- 1% say they have talked on the air in the last month or

Total Respondents: 1507

Percent Saying Each Is A "Major Reason" They Listen To Program			
	Total	Regular Listeners	Callers
Respondents (N=)	951	277	113
To learn about how different people feel about different issues	71%	85%	83%
To keep up on issues of the day	70%	84%	78%
Because it is a good way to learn things that I can't find out elsewhere	58%	68%	62%
Because it is entertaining	40%	50%	44%
I pick up information that I use in conversation with other people	33%	45%	33%
Because I like the host of the show	27%	39%	38%

1993 Talk Radio Survey (cont.)
Times Mirror Center for the People and the Press

	Percent Saying "Talk Radio Hosts" Are More Liberal/Conservative Than They Are				
	More Liberal	More Conservative	The Same	Mixed/ No Opinion	N
Total	**33%**	**19%**	**37%**	**11%**	**951**
Talk Radio					
Regular Listeners	33%	17%	40%	10%	277
Callers	38%	16%	37%	9%	113
Party ID					
Democratic	24%	25%	42%	10%	280
Independent	35%	19%	33%	13%	321
Republican	41%	13%	37%	10%	308
Ideology					
Liberal	20%	30%	43%	7%	118
In Between	27%	23%	39%	11%	533
Conservative	52%	7%	30%	11%	280
Presidential Vote					
Clinton	20%	29%	38%	13%	282
Perot	35%	16%	39%	11%	146
Bush	44%	11%	32%	14%	253

Percent Saying Each Is A "Critical" Issue			
	Talk Hosts	Regular Listeners	General Public
Respondents (N=)	112	227	1507
Improving public education	76%	49%	49%
Economic conditions	72%	55%	53%
Reducing the deficit	63%	57%	48%
Dealing with homelessness	12%	27%	33%
Protecting the environment	15%	25%	34%
Abortion	11%	23%	21%

1992 Political Advertising Survey
Paragon Research, April 1992
427 adults were surveyed who listened to radio at least an hour a day

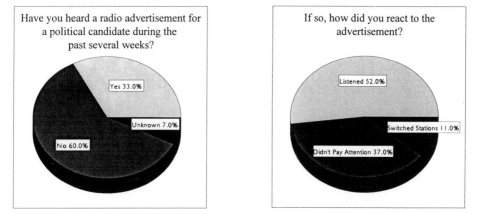

Have you heard a radio advertisement for a political candidate during the past several weeks?

Yes 33.0%
Unknown 7.0%
No 60.0%

If so, how did you react to the advertisement?

Listened 52.0%
Switched Stations 11.0%
Didn't Pay Attention 37.0%

Using a 1-10 scale, respondents answered the following questions.
1= Disagree Completely   10= Agree Completely

"Political ads on the radio help me make an informed choice about who to vote for."
38% Disagreed Completely   Average 3.3   <4% Agreed Completely

"Political ads on the radio are as effective as political ads in a newspaper when it comes to informing me about political candidates."
>25% Disagreed Completely   Average 4.2   <8% Agreed Completely

"Radio stations should not air any political ads."
>38% Disagreed Completely   Average 3.9   16% Agreed Completely

Political Party Preference			
	Total	Men	Women
Republican	40%	38%	43%
Democrat	28%	27%	29%
Independent	18%	29%	16%
Didn't Know/Refused	14%	15%	12%

Appendix

INTERVIEW CONFIRMATION

DATE:

TIME:

STATION:

HOST:

PRODUCER/CONTACT:

GUEST:

TITLF:

LENGTH OF INTERVIEW:

LIVE/TAPED:

CALL IN?   **LINE #1**
                  LINE #2

PHONER/IN STUDIO?

SHOW PHONE #:

EMERGENCY PHONE #:

NEWMAN COMMUNICATIONS, INC.
Schedule of Interviews for Dave Olive
More Political Babble

Friday, April 18, 1996

6

TIME:	6:35 a.m.
STATION:	WBZS-AM, Alexandria, VA
HOST:	Steve Chiconas
STUDIO #:	202-289-7730
STATION #:	703-683-3000
COMMENTS:	5 min. Live, you will call the studio number

7

TIME:	6:45 a.m.
STATION:	WOOD-AM Grand Rapids MI
HOST:	Gary Allen
STUDIO #:	616-774-2008
STATION #:	616-459-1919
COMMENTS:	5 min. Live. Main talk station.

8

TIME:	7:10 a.m.
STATION:	WKDR-AM, Burlington, VT
HOST:	Louis Manno
STUDIO #:	800-286-9537
STATION #:	802-862-8255
COMMENTS:	15 min. Live. Top talk station.

9

TIME:	7:25 a.m.
STATION:	WDRC-AM, Hartford, CT
HOST:	Jim Rayner
STUDIO #:	860-243-8413
STATION #:	860-243-1115
COMMENTS:	10 min. Live

DEMOCRATIC ★ NATIONAL ★ COMMITTEE
David Wilhelm, Chairman

March 3, 1994

The Honorable Newt Gingrich
2428 Rayburn House Office Building
Washington, DC 20515

Dear Representative Gingrich:

Congratulations! You are a recipient of the 1994 "Chicken Little"
award for your misguided and outrageous predictions about President
Clinton's plan to rebuild the economy.

Today, the economy is on the rebound. Job growth is up.
Unemployment and interest rates are down. Consumers and
businesses alike are taking advantage of the improved economic
prospects.

This, I suspect, comes as a surprise to you. Your comments last
year during the debate on the President's budget made it very clear
you thought the President's plan to invest in our people while
cutting the deficit was the wrong prescription for a sick economy.

Millions of Americans in every region of the country are now
benefitting from the economic recovery. While there is much work
to be done, we have made real progress.

I hope we can count on you to play a constructive role in our
continuing efforts to improve the lives of America's hard working
families. Join us in looking forward instead of looking for the
sky to fall.

Sincerely,

David Wilhelm
Chairman

Democratic Party Headquarters • 430 South Capitol Street, S.E. • Washington, D.C. 20003 • 202.863.8000 • FAX: 202.863.8091
Paid for by the Democratic National Committee. Contributions to the Democratic National Committee are not tax deductible.

The 1994 Chicken Little Award

This certificate is hereby awarded to

Representative Newt Gingrich

for inaccurate predictions of gloom and disaster, and a lack of hope, confidence and willingness to make good things happen for the American people.

CONGRESSMAN

Joel Hefley

2351 Rayburn H.O.B.
Washington, D.C. 20515-0605
(202) 225-4422

FOR IMMEDIATE RELEASE

CONTACT Leigh S. LaMora
(202) 225-4422

"PORKER OF THE WEEK" AWARD

(Washington, D C -- January 3, 1996)"Taxpayers have forked over 1.3 billion dollars for a stretch of highway that's still not completed -- 35 years after the work first began

"Apparently, back in 1960, 70 million dollars was budgeted for the 'H3' on Oahu, Hawaii. The Defense Department's Army Corps of Engineers planned a 16-mile, six lane highway to move military equipment and troops across the island to Pearl Harbor to be shipped to Vietnam.

"But a series of setbacks forced long delays Work stopped for 17 years while protesters successfully prevented the highway from cutting through a rain forest New, re-drawn plans forced the relocation of a large animal quarantine center Ancient burial grounds were uncovered, and the list goes on and on

"With three miles left to go, it's estimated the H3 will cost more than 1.3 billion dollars -- which is 70 million dollars a mile, or 19 times the original estimate   The Defense Department expects to complete H3 by 1997

"After all these years, one has to wonder if this six lane highway is a necessary taxpayer expense The Department of Defense gets my 'Porker of the Week' Award "

-30-

F E N T O N
C O M M U N I
C A T I O N S

1606 20th ST. NW

WASH. DC 20009

TEL:202/745-0707

FAX:202/332-1915

I N T E R N E T
fenton@fenton.com

A Fax from Fenton Communications

MIKE PETERS/Dayton Daily News

Celia Rocks Communications

May 15, 1996

Mr. Doug Stephan, Host
"Good Day, USA"
% Stephan Productions
1084 Grove Street
Framingham, MA 01701

Dear Doug:

Just a quick note to thank you for booking Karen Leland, author of "Customer Service For Dummies", on the "Live Line" segment of your program. You did a great job of getting to the key issues, and the interview was fast-paced and informative.

Ms. Leland said that the interview went so well and you received so many calls from interested listeners that your producer also booked her on your evening program on KABC in Los Angeles.

Everyone on our end was very excited about the success of the interview. I look forward to working with you again in the future -- booking more hot topics and best-selling authors on your program.

Sincerely,

Celia Rocks

Celia Rocks

A Guide to Spotting a Phony Environmentalist in Congress

Graduation Cap: Speaks at your kid's graduation about protecting the future, but votes to gut laws that protect the next generation's health and safety.

Sapling: Plants a tree on Arbor Day, but votes to clear-cut our national forests.

Binoculars: Used not for watching rare birds on vital wetlands, but to survey their home for a big contributor's next strip mall.

Money: Don't be fooled; these greenbacks are campaign dollars from his polluter friends.

Hiking Boots: These boots are made for walking...with the CEO of a mining company that just bought a National Park.

Recycle Pin: Gives lip service to recycli programs in public, then votes in Washin to cut funds for conservation.

Zoo Pin: Good thing he supports the local zoo; it's the only place you'll see many of those animals after he guts the Endangered Species Act.

Shooting Glasses: Used for ducl hunting, until he voted to let developers pave over the last wetland (see binoculars).

How-to Memo: You too can Greenscam: This memo teaches everything about looking like ar environmentalist on Earth Day, while voting to gut environment protections.

Trash: Collects garbage at a beach clean-up for local TV, th votes to gut the Clean Water A that protects beaches, rivers ar lakes year 'round.

Designed by The November Group
for The Environmental Information Center.
Washington, D.C., 1996.

May 21, 1996

Jack Sunday
KFGO-AM
1020 South 25th Street
Fargo, ND 58108

100 Medway Road, Suite 203

Milford, MA 01757

Telephone: 508.478.0900

FAX: 508.478.4410

Dear Jack:

No item on this year's political agenda will be as hotly contested--and as important to the long-term direction of the country--as the Balanced Budget Amendment. Requiring the government to live within its means will dramatically, directly impact every level of American society.

And while everyone supports a balanced budget, **The National Committee to Preserve Social Security and Medicare** knows that this current Amendment is seriously flawed--and will force Congress to rob billions of dollars in retirement funds to pay for a federal deficit slush fund.

"By themselves, Social Security and a balanced budget are great ideas. But together, they're a recipe for financial disaster. The proposed constitutional amendment would rely ever more heavily on the annual surpluses of the Social Security trust funds--payroll taxes paid by working Americans--to offset the huge deficit in the general revenue fund," comments **National Committee** president Martha McSteen.

With six million members from across the country, the grassroots-oriented **National Committee** is determined to keep a Balanced Budget Amendment which includes Social Security from ever becoming part of the Constitution of the United States, and to emerge victorious in this most important of political battles.

You won't have an interview which will spark debate, and light up the phones, like a segment with an executive from **The National Committee**. They are proven, sure-fire winners on talk radio throughout the country, including stations such as:

KMOX, WJR, WLS, WBAP, KRLD, KCBS, WBUR, WCCO, KOA, WTMJ, WOAI, WPOP, WPBR, WRC, WHYY, KSFO, KTAR, KTOK, and National Public Radio.

The National Committee provides some of the best guests in talk radio. A segment with one of their executives isn't peppered with people complaining ab out their last Social Security check; rather, *an interview with a National Committee executive invariably becomes a red-hot debate about politics, power, and the way our country ought to be governed.* You'll never see callers get so fired up.

In an interview, **The National Committee's** representative will discuss:

• **Why someone who supports a balanced budget shouldn't favor this flawed Amendment;**

• **The importance of protecting people's retirement money from Congressional pork-barrelers;**

• **Why the Balanced Budget Amendment is an important issue for everyone--not just** seniors;

• How Congress currently uses your Social Security retirement funds to hide the true size of the federal deficit;

• The current status of the Amendment;

• The impact of the Balanced Budget Amendment on average families in your area;

• What your audience can do to participate in the Balanced Budget debate.

Martha A. McSteen become President of **The National Committee to Preserve Social Security and Medicare** in 1989 after a distinguished 39-year career with the Social Security Administration. Appointed by President Reagan in 1983 to head the Administration, she served as acting commissioner for three years. During her tenure, she overhauled the retirement and disability insurance program and dramatically improved the Administration's work in child support enforcement and debt collection.

Max Richtman, **The National Committee's** Executive Vice President, is a respected Capitol Hill veteran. A former staff director for the Senate Special Committee on Aging and the Senate Select Committee on Indian Affairs, Richtman directed a lengthy investigation of the Equal Opportunity Commission and played key roles in reforms of the multi-billion dollar Indian energy and Health care systems.

The National Committee's Director of Public Affairs Bill Ritz began his impressive journalistic career in radio, and later worked for The Associated Press and for The Denver Post, where he earned the Heywood Broun and George Polk Awards for excellence in journalism. After three years as a speech writer for Phillips Petroleum, Ritz moved to Capitol Hill, serving as director of communications for the Senate Special Committee on Aging.

The Balanced Budget Amendment is today's most explosive political issue. Its current version would jeopardize money invested for decades to ensure the very American--both young and old--won't spend their golden years in poverty. **The National Committee** is committed to making sure such a flawed Amendment never gets ratified. And this unique position from the organization's media-savvy, entertaining executives has made for hit, timely talk on radio stations throughout the country.

To schedule a powerful, controversial interview with an executive from **The National Committee to Preserve Social Security and Medicare,** or for more information about the group, please contact me at **(508) 478-0900**.

Sincerely,

Robert K. Newman
President

A

Abortion, 35, 90
Actuality line, 56
Advertising, 19
Advocacy organizations, 112
African-Americans, 37
AIDS, 30, 82
Albl, Michael, 102
Alcoholics Anonymous, 117
America Online, 130
Americans for Separation of
    Church and State, 19, 112
Americans for Tax Reform, 80
Asner, Ed, 50
Assertiveness training, 69
Associated Press, 76

B

Bag of options, 106
Baird, Zoe, 39
Balanced budget, 79
Ball, Lucille, 39
Barbour, Haley, 55
Bell, Art, 74
Blaming the media, 104
BMW, 45
Body language, 110, 120, 121,
    122, 142
Bohannon, Jim, 19, 114
Bosnia, 37
Boston Red Sox, 115
Breast implants, 112
Briefing memo, 52
Budget crisis, 80
Buick, 50
Byrne, Jay, 93

C

Call waiting, 68
Caller ID, 67
Canada, 37
Caplan, Aric, 40, 50
Car phones, 66
Career patrons, 43
Catch phrase, 42
Center for Constitutional
    Rights, 65

Center for Public Integrity, 43
Chamber of Commerce, 64
Chicago Seven, 61
Chicken Little Award, 54
Christian stations, 74
Clinton Administration, 111
Clinton voters, 34
Clinton, Bill, 17, 32, 35, 43, 48,
    98, 105
Common denominator, 33
Communities, 16
Competition, 70
Complex situations, 37
Compressed conflicts, 43
Compuserve, 130
Conference calls, 79
Congress, 34, 41, 44
Controversy, 80
Corvette, 50
Creating a message, 30
Credibility, 100, 101, 112, 121
Critical Mass Media, 102
Cultivating relationships, 85
Current events, 38
Cyberspace, 130

D

D'Amato, Alphonse, 31
Databases, 82
Debates, 71, 110
Defining issues, 30
Delphi, 130
Democratic Leadership Council,
    60
Democratic National
    Committee, 54, 66
Democratic National
    Convention, 61
Democrats, 46, 52, 55, 86, 99,
    135
Demographics, 29, 32, 45, 67,
    81
Disclosure of funding sources,
    111
Dole, Bob, 33, 35, 52, 113
Drive time, 29